SandStory

SandStory

the amazing tale

of how sand

changed my life

Joe Castillo

WestBow·
PRESS
A DIVISION OF THOMAS NELSON
& ZONDERVAN

WestBow Press books may be ordered through booksellers or by contacting:

WestBow Press
A Division of Thomas Nelson & Zondervan
1663 Liberty Drive
Bloomington, IN 47403
www.westbowpress.com
1 (866) 928-1240

Because of the dynamic nature of the Internet, any web addresses or
links contained in this book may have changed since publication and
may no longer be valid. The views expressed in this work are solely those
of the author and do not necessarily reflect the views of the publisher,
and the publisher hereby disclaims any responsibility for them.

ISBN: 978-1-4908-2310-2 (sc)
ISBN: 978-1-4908-2309-6 (hc)
ISBN: 978-1-4908-2311-9 (e)

Library of Congress Control Number: 2014901439

Printed in the United States of America.

WestBow Press rev. date: 1/27/2014

Acknowledgments

God gets top billing. *SandStory*, this book and all the good things that have transpired in this marvelous chain of events, all originated in the mind of God. Solomon, king of Israel, said it best: "There is nothing new under the sun." Everything that appears to be original, fresh, or new is really just a rehash of something God thought up before the origins of time. We just get to be amazed at His infinite creativity and thrilled when He allows us to be a part of revealing it to the world.

Almost at the same level is "Saint Cindy," my wife of many years, who was in on the very beginnings of my SandStory dabbling. Since then, she has carried the weight of the joys, sorrows, and frustrations of being married to an artist. Cindy has also carried the suitcases with our clothing and merchandise, the marketing material briefcase, the display sign, the credit card machine, the money bag, the excess cables, the first aid kit, chargers, attachments, Dentyne, Chap Stick, lotion, hand sanitizer, and about a thousand other things that only fit in her purse, because it opens into another dimension, just like Hermione Granger's in the Harry Potter books. She literally amazes me every day. This book is written in the first person, but that in no way minimizes the second person who has been involved in every word, line, and editorial change.

A third person in the mix is my son José. Creativity oozes out of every pore of this guy's body, the way the odor of chili peppers will when you eat too many of them. José really started it all by sending me the first little YouTube clip. He also gave me terrific marketing advice, as well as the names, words, and slogans that I have continued to use with great success. He has been the geek and technical hotline for every sort of problem, and he solves them all with the same ease he exhibits in tossing together great meals.

Feared and revered professor from Sam Houston State University, my brilliant sister, Dr. Caroline Crimm—an accomplished author in her own right—was known by those who feared her as the "Crimm Reaper." Those who loved her (far greater in number than the first group) knew she was the sharpest pencil in the box. With more than thirty years of teaching and correcting the errors of sophomoric, fledgling writers, she was the logical choice to be editor of my meandering *SandStory*. Any spit, polish, and shine that glows from these pages was put there thanks to her keen eye to detail. Any errors—grammatical, spelling, or otherwise—indubitably remain because I deviated from her precise red marks or ignored them at my peril. Thanks, Sis, for all your help and encouragement. Other corrections and input came from Pauline Hitt, longtime English teacher, and the crack editorial staff at Westbow Press; Nathaniel Best and Brandon Grew. Thanks also to the design talents of Jessica Mansell and Kata Teuton.

All the rest of my family deserve endless thanks for encouraging, supporting, cheering, voting, and believing that I could really pull this thing off.

My mom, Martha Lou Gorton Castillo, embodies all this. Her artistic instruction when I was still too young to talk, her fabulous stories acted out at parties and family get-togethers, and her can-do spirit, even at ninety-four—all of those things still inspire me. Mom attended the very first "official" SandStory performance in Marco Island, Florida, and will enthrall anyone who gets within the sound of her voice with stories of her famous son.

Daughters Maria and Jennifer and son Bryan have endured being without our presence as parents and grandparents at many birthday parties, celebrations, and holidays. I love them for their patience and willingness to wait.

Last, but in no way least, is Tim Grable. That stalwart of negotiation skills, paragon of booking abilities, champion marketer, and indefatigable worker undoubtedly took my SandStory career to heights I never would have known. I am also confident that the entire tale has not yet been told. At some point, because of Tim, there might be *SandStory Part II: The Further Adventures of Joe and Cindy Castillo.*

To all, from the bottom of my heart, thank you! !

CONTENTS

CHAPTER ONE

NOTHING WASTED

God Uses Even Insignificant Parts of Our Lives

Everyone will share the story of your wonderful goodness ...
—Psalm 145:7

This is the amazing tale of how sand changed my life. Let me start at the beginning.

I love a good story. The very first story I can remember reading all by myself was *The Little Engine That Could* by Mary C. Jacobs. It was a clever motivational book with all the elements of a great story. It had drama, tension, conflict, an engaging protagonist, and a fine resolution. There was nothing in the book that was unnecessary. I have read plenty of books since that were a lot worse.

Usually the biggest problem with a bad book is including stuff that is unnecessary—pointless descriptions that go on and on, extraneous characters, unconnected plotlines, and more. A really memorable story includes all of the information you need and nothing you don't. It snags you at the beginning and leaves you feeling satisfied at the end.

It connects all the dots. My fascination with stories has influenced almost every part of my life. In my work, in my relationships, in my art, I have always wanted to find and include the story. I have also come to the conclusion that God does too.

Our Common Dilemma

If you examine my life from the outside, it doesn't seem to read like a well-written story. It appears to wander as it includes, people, and events that don't make sense in the grand scheme of things. Part of my lifelong belief structure has always included the concept that God is in control. He, I am convinced, directs every life. But if God is the author of my story, it doesn't seem that He has done a very good job. Too many things don't make sense. More authors and speakers than I can count have tried to explain why God does things and how we are supposed to genially approve of His doings, sort of a fledgling actor taking pointers from the veteran director.

I think most people, if they were honest, would agree that much in their lives just doesn't make sense. The real truth is that once you have been around the block a few times, if you see things through spiritual eyes, the story starts to come together. You can see a purpose in random events. It also keeps you wanting to know what comes next.

All the Pieces

Now more than ever, I firmly believe that God does not include anything in our lives that is unnecessary. Every detail is of value and part of the story. All of our joys, all of our sorrows, the successes, and even the failures make up a compelling narrative that becomes our lives. Someday we will read it from beginning to end and be very satisfied with the results. I promised I would tell you how I became a SandStory artist, but first you have to understand how the parts fell into place.

Way Back at the Beginning

I am introduced as an artist, but it is really not my fault. My mother is an artist, my father was an artist, my aunt Caroline Fuller was an accomplished portrait painter, and I even had an uncle named Artie. I'm sure my first solid food was Crayola crayons. My family hung around with well-known Mexican artists, some of whom became world famous. When I was six, my mother taught me and a handful of neighborhood kids in a community art class. When I was twelve, my father instructed me in the art of brush lettering. In high school, I carried a sketch pad and got attention by doing sketches of my friends. My favorite pickup line was, "Hi, would you mind if I do a quick sketch of you?" I spent more time in museums and art galleries than Michelangelo spent painting the Sistine Chapel. Art played a huge role in my formative years.

Significant Moments

One of the great significant times in my life came when I was fourteen. Invited to a church camp, I heard for the very first time that Jesus Christ loved me and died on the cross to forgive my sins. I heard that by faith in Him, I not only received forgiveness, but He also gave me the power to live a new life and the assurance of eternity in heaven. A Christian chalk artist presented that message, and I accepted it eagerly.

Despite the pervasive artistic influence in my background and my new love for Christ, by the time I got to art school, I was thoroughly convinced that all the great Christian artwork had already been done. I didn't want to compete with Michelangelo, Leonardo, Raphael, or Donatello. They were all great Renaissance painters, which I remember only because they are also the names of the four Ninja Turtles. And I didn't want to do velvet paintings of Jesus, although I have seen some very good ones.

Adventures in Commercial Art

Ringling School of Art in Sarasota, Florida, was an eye-opening experience. There were two tracks: fine art and commercial art. The most important lesson I learned there was that if you go into fine art, you will be broke, hungry, have to live in a dingy attic apartment, and before you can receive any acclaim for all your painstaking effort and sacrifice, you have to cut your ear off and die. It didn't sound like my idea of a great life. The fine artists would say, superciliously, "I want people to pay me for what springs from my soul." The commercial artists would say, "I want to pay the rent." Obviously, commercial art became my choice. Before I started my career, though, I spent five years in Bible college, got married, and went to Mexico as a missionary for two years. That is another story I may write about later.

The Challenge Begins

I wanted to make a living as a commercial artist. There is an easy way and there is a hard way. Not knowing any better, I chose the latter. Instead of going to work for someone else and learning from the bottom up, I launched out on my own. My business card said, with brash cockiness, "CASTILLO ADVERTISING: Art, Graphics, Copy, Public Relations." I knew some of the business from my dad, God in His mercy had given me a moderate amount of talent, and almost every college activity and part-time job down through the years had included some form of visual art.

Furthermore, failure was not an option. A wife and two small children to feed, clothe, and house is great motivation. But competition was stiff in Knoxville, Tennessee, so I had to be flexible. My motto became, "Sure, I can do that."

Over the next eighteen years, I took almost any job that came along. The typical commercial stuff like logo designs, brochures, and catalogs were the bread and butter. The "not-so-typical" included brush-lettering signs, pastel portraits, courtroom drawings, airbrushing T-shirts, clay modeling, and three-dimensional displays. Some of those adventures were bizarre enough to fill yet another book.

A Wake-Up Call

Eventually, flexibility and hard work paid off. Castillo Advertising became the Advertising Library, with its own building and thirteen employees. Running an advertising agency was really not my best fit. The creative part, which was being done more and more by others, had energized me. The administrative part sucked me dry. The stress of not really listening to God's promptings and following Him began to take its toll. Chest pains and sleepless nights alerted me that some changes had to be made.

It was around then that I got a phone call from my pastor, John Stone. John wanted me to put together a "chalk talk," an art presentation for our church's Christmas program. I knew what they were; it was exactly that kind of presentation that had brought me to Christ.

Perhaps it was arrogance—or more likely fear of failure—that prompted my response. "John, I don't have the right chalks or a large easel; I have never done one of those, and I really don't do Christian art." Thinking that was the end of it, I felt the subject was closed. John, tenacious John, was not having any of that. "Joe," he said, sounding a little testy, "you are a Christian, and you are an artist. Do *something*." So I reluctantly agreed. No chalks, no large easel, and no experience pushed me again to my advertising motto, "I can do that." I felt a little like Moses when God asked him, "What do you have in your hand?" (Exodus 4:2)

I had large four-foot rolls of newsprint and Magic Markers in abundance around my studio, so the result was a "Magic Marker talk." The drawing that came from that first effort I later called "The Face of Christ." I drew the story of the life of Christ. The details combined at the end to form the image of His face. Putting the eyes and nose in at the very last created an "Aha!" moment that gave the presentation some drama.

Opening My Eyes

The drawing went much better than I expected, with many people afterward asking for copies. Producing a pen-and-ink rendering, printing copies, and handing them out was no problem for someone in advertising. It was at that point I seemed to lose control of my life. Business was not going well. The chest pains were increasing. Someone else copyrighted the Face of Christ drawing and was selling it without paying royalties, and my wife developed breast cancer.

What happened next was a story worth retelling. I wrote it all down in my first book, *The Face of Christ*, which, if you are interested, is available at my website, *JoeCastillo.com*. It is worth reading because it is a God story. Difficult times are the ones that teach us the most. I learned obedience to God's prompting, the importance of forgiveness, and how God can use a simple line drawing of the Face of Christ to change lives. It was an amazing experience, but there was much more to come. This was my very first "ArtStory."

Putting It All Together

Fast forward a few turbulent decades, during which my wife went home to be with the Lord, I sold my business, went back to seminary, got a degree, remarried to a wonderful gal named Cindy, and started pastoring a church. Looking back on all of that gave me the perspective to see that God's providence and gentle guidance were including all of the strands in the warp and woof of my personal tapestry. The story was starting to make sense. My birth, cultural background, artistic ventures, and struggles all were coming together to form what I could now see as a masterpiece of His creativity: a magnum opus that included purpose in every color, every shade and tone, every stroke of His delicate brush.

Fertile Soil

With all of this history and experience swirling around in my mind, art became central in planting a new church. The arts had been a huge part of my life; it was in my DNA code. My parents had given me a love for it. The artist who brought me to Christ had shared the story of Christ's forgiveness with me through art. Dozens of advertising projects using photography, animation, live sketching, graphic demonstrations, and illustrations taught me to use my hands in high-pressure, time-sensitive situations. I had learned about obedience and forgiveness and mercy because of my drawing of the face of Christ. It only made sense that I wanted to blend art into the colors of a vibrant new church.

I was also very aware that this is a visual generation, and using the arts was the logical way to reach them. Our services at Northridge Church became a gallery of artwork in every medium you can imagine. We used PowerPoint, paintings, pastels, marker drawings, sculptures, videos, movie clips, and cartoons. It was great fun!

As the church grew, we moved into and remodeled an old movie theater that still had the large screen. All of our art creations could be projected larger than life. We tried to stay fresh and creative, but when you are doing things on a weekly basis, it's a huge challenge. The creative element became a stretch. After almost five years, I was running out of ideas. The two biggest times for church attendance are Christmas and Easter. With Easter coming up, I needed something new.

CHAPTER TWO

HOW IT ALL STARTED

The Beginning of SandStory

For I am about to do a brand new thing.
See, I have already begun! Do you not see it?
—Isaiah 43:19

A Grainy Little Video Clip

*M*y son, José, is every bit as creative as I am and much more talented. His area of expertise, though, had become that new art form called the Internet. Plunked down right at the intersection of marketing, technology, and creativity, he was on the cutting edge and spent a lot of time online.

One day in April, he ran across a short, grainy clip of an artist named Kako creating images in sand for an animators' event in Korea. It caught my son's eye, and he sent it along to me as an e-mail attachment with the cryptic note, "Dad, you need to give this a try." It was the right time, and since I was looking for a new idea for church, it was the right place.

A Humble Experiment

The next week, Cindy sent me off to buy some mulch for the garden. Wandering through Lowe's is a dangerous experience for me. I am always mesmerized by the plethora of tools, gadgets, widgets, and materials that are stacked almost to the top of forty-five-foot ceilings. I can do serious damage to my credit card account in just a few minutes.

What was on my mind on that trip was our Easter church service. We needed a fresh way of telling an old story. I should have been in the garden section, looking for mulch, but I was just cruising. As I strolled down the aisle that included bags of sand, I noticed one of the bags had been ripped open and spilled out on the concrete floor. White sand on dark concrete. Shoppers had scuffed through the sand, leaving lines and patterns.

Artists have a natural tendency to see images everywhere. I am no exception. In the scuff marks, I could see shapes and images. Then I started dragging the toe of my sneaker through the sand. I got home with the mulch, but I also had a trunk full of gear, including a bag of sand, a kitchen light fixture, a piece of glass, four table legs, some one-by-fours, and various nuts and screws. I started "MacGyvering" my first sand table out of this collection of parts in my garage.

The story is important, but one of the key elements in any public performance is building the drama. Sand images started appearing on my homemade sand table, and I wanted to add some drama to it in the form of music. What kind of music would go well with a story told in sand? Cindy, my clever wife, occasionally wandered out to the garage to bring sustenance and check on my contraption. I shared my concern for finding the right music. Practical and ever helpful, she mentioned the powerful music we had just heard watching Mel Gibson's movie, *The Passion of the Christ*. The visuals in the film were so intense, the music was often overshadowed and forgotten.

After purchasing a CD of the soundtrack, I found it was perfect. Composed by the masterful John Debney, it inspired images that came together for the very first SandStory, which I called "The Passion."

To get the images on the screen, I duct-taped a portable Handycam to a tripod and plugged it into our church projector, and voilá! There was the sand, my hands, and any images I wanted to draw, projected huge up on the screen.

The Very First Performance

Although I am very prone to just wing it, it seemed like a good idea to try out my SandStory experiment before performing for our congregation. We invited a couple dozen folks from the church to come over Saturday night for a dress rehearsal. Setting up my wobbly kitchen light fixture/table on stage for the first time seemed pretty crazy to me, but at that point I was, well, committed. Getting the tripod in place was tricky. The lights went down, the music started, and the image came up on the screen. I realized we had a problem: the image was upside down.

Handycams generally do not have an attachment on both the top and bottom, so the tripod had to be behind me, instead of in front of the table. We commandeered a boom attachment from a mike stand, so that the arm would be long enough to reach over my head, duct-taped the camera to it, and we started the performance again. Things started fine, but a few minutes into the performance, the camera—which was old and heavy—began to sag. The image on the screen grew larger and larger, until the contraption bumped me on the head. I tightened the arm with a pair of pliers and supported it with yards of duct tape.

I started again. We progressed right up to the tense moment of the crucifixion, when suddenly, *blink*, the screen went dark. Handycams, in case you don't know, will go to sleep if you are not recording. I was not, and it did. After all the technical glitches, Easter Sunday morning, believe it or not, went off without a hitch. My congregation overflowed with lavish accolades. But they were my congregation They were supposed to say nice things about the sermons and my crazy art projects.

Unexpected Help

It seems that many good ideas need gestational time before they hatch. The first SandStory was developed for Easter Sunday of 2004, but it was a long time before our first live performance. Cindy and I had stepped down from pastoring the church and were sort of at loose ends. We accepted a temporary position, offered graciously by my friend, Paul Cowell, at his lovely Whitestone Country Inn, just outside of Kingston, Tennessee. He has helped me out on a number of occasions. I set up my wobbly, homemade light table in the attic of one of the B&B's buildings and filmed my first and only SandStory, "The Passion."

The birthing process sometimes requires a midwife. Almost one year after our Easter performance, a friend I had gotten to know at Asbury Seminary called. The seminary was having a president's retreat on Marco Island, Florida, and they wanted me to come and perform my new SandStory art. It sounded very exciting.

For two weeks, I practiced like a madman. Then I shipped my "Rube Goldberg" table via UPS in a cardboard box, and Cindy and I hopped on a plane. When my table showed up, the cardboard box was in shreds, the glass was broken, and the whole deal was more rickety than ever.

Fortunately for us, Asbury Seminary has one of the most sophisticated media centers of any school in the United States. When Doug Penix, who was setting up the technical aspect of the retreat, got a look at my pile of shards, wires, and duct tape, he smiled like a NASA scientist checking out his grandson's garbage-can rocket ship.

"Hey, Joe," he said, "why don't you let us help you with that?"

By the time they were done, his team had replaced the glass, reinforced my lame table, and built a frame overhead, holding one of their high-definition cameras. It was like moving up to the Major Leagues.

A Defining Moment

Later that evening, as the lights dimmed, John Debney's gripping music started. Played through state-of-the-art speakers, the music rumbled the floor and vibrated the chandeliers. Every grain of sand was in sharp focus on two giant screens. The images began unfolding under my fingers in the darkened auditorium. Even though I am always laser-focused on my hand motions, about halfway through my performance, I noticed the room had become abnormally still. The hair on the back of my neck stood up, my face tingled, and goose bumps rose on my arms. In some way I could not understand, the spirit of God was at work. It was very much as if all the air had been sucked from the room. The face of the resurrected Christ holding out His pierced hand as evidence to doubting Thomas was my final image. The last haunting chord faded into silence. I stepped away from the table. Nobody breathed.

As the lights came up, many seemed to be wiping tears from their cheeks. A softly breathed "Oh my!" from the back loosened the tension with a collective exhalation. Never before or since have I experienced the power and intensity of a moment in that way. In the silence, God seemed to be saying, "This is the way. Walk in it."

Accolades

Being on stage is not new to me. Public speaking class in high school was an easy A. Hundreds of hours teaching classes, giving lectures and sermons had placed me frequently in the public eye. The audiences have always been more generous in their appreciative words than I deserved, but nothing I had ever experienced prepared me for that moment at the Asbury Seminary retreat.

A very well-known and accomplished speaker followed the SandStory performance. He struggled to refocus the audience but failed badly. As soon as he was done, I was surrounded by a hundred or so people, all wanting to shake my hand and offer some form of praise. The comments I kept hearing were things like: *Wow, that is the most powerful thing I have ever seen! Incredible! Captivating! Absolutely unique! I have never seen anything like that before! I just couldn't control the tears! Bless you, you have touched my life in a way nothing ever has.*

All I could do was look into the eyes of person after person and say, "Thank you, thank you, thank you." What kept going through my mind was, *How do you let people know that the guy pushing the sand around was not responsible for the power that had permeated the room?* I was convinced that it was a divine miracle. Not on the level of parting the Red Sea or bringing water out of a rock, but nonetheless something for which I could not claim responsibility. Since that day, many people have expressed similar emotions, leaving me with but one conclusion: God can and often does choose the most humble and insignificant tools to accomplish His work. After all, it is just sand.

The Phone Starts Ringing

Regardless of the beautiful place and all the adulation, my wife and I still had jobs back in Tennessee, so we headed home. Not really knowing what would happen next, I filed the entire experience under the heading of "great stories to tell my grandkids." However, the very next day, the phone rang again. Dr. Joe Mclarin from Carillon United Methodist Church in Orlando, Florida, was the first.

"Joe, we really would love to have you perform for us here in Florida."

I had to say no. By the time summer rolled around, I had turned down several requests a month. Cindy and I looked at each other and asked, "Well, do you think we could make a living just doing sand art?"

It is a very comforting thing, having a job with a regular paycheck. The thought of jumping off the cliff and taking the entire endeavor by faith was not new to either of us. At different times, we had both accepted a call to the mission field without a guaranteed salary. Missionary work is a noble and respected profession. But sand art? Really? Who in the world is making it as a sand artist?

By the time November rolled around, we had decided we were going to give it a try. One of the deciding factors was that our home in Richmond, Kentucky, had been on the market for almost two years without even a serious nibble. It was time to go home. Call it a leap of faith or sheer, unadulterated lunacy, we were going to take the plunge.

CHAPTER THREE

TABLES, TINKERING, AND TECHNOLOGY

Getting It All to Work Right

They selected young men that were respected, skillful in all wisdom and clever in knowledge and understanding science.
—Daniel 1:4

Table Number Two

The rickety table first conceived in Lowe's and assembled in my garage worked for a few performances, but we needed to have something reliable that would travel. Now that we were serious about going on the road, the job of finding someone who could help me build a table again fell upon my son, José. A display company that employed some of his friends seemed a likely group. The next time we stopped in Johnson City, Tennessee, where he and his wife Shannon lived, we trotted down to Essex, Inc. We exchanged drawings and ideas, and they went to work. About three weeks later, they called, saying it was ready for inspection.

They replaced the fragile fluorescent kitchen light fixture with state-of-the-art LED lights in three colors, with adjustable rheostats. Wells on either side held the excess sand, and this sturdy SandStory T2 folded up and fit in a shipping case with handle and wheels. It all was very cool. The guys who built it had never seen SandStory before, so a short performance in their warehouse gave them an appreciation for how their handiwork would be used.

The T2 was a fantastic improvement. We dragged it around, set it up, and used it for more than a year. I performed some of those early events in more than thirty elementary schools in central Kentucky. I had begun doing SandStories of creation with all the fish, animals, and birds, along with some other new pieces. We arrived, set up in the gym or auditorium, and the principal with the help of the teachers ushered in about two to three hundred overactive children. Inevitably, the warnings and disclaimers would start.

"Now, Mr. Castillo, these are very young children. They don't behave very well in large groups, so don't take it personally if they are rambunctious during your presentation. They are just kids being kids."

As soon as the music started and the first image appeared on the screen, the kids fell silent. For the next thirty minutes, you could hear the proverbial pin drop. The reactions got to be quite comical. Mouths hanging open, the astonished teachers said, "How did you *do* that?"

I just shrugged and said, "That is the power of the arts."

T2 was a great workhorse. It only had one serious problem. Constructed from laminated wood with black Formica covering, it weighed two hundred pounds. Trying to lug it up and down steps and loading into the back of my SUV was brutal. Cindy and I together could manage it, but we were eventually going to give ourselves hernias. Not only that, when we began traveling long distances, the only way T2 could get there was by shipping it on a truck.

At our first event on the West Coast, we had to put it on a skid and ship it via a freight carrier. When we got out to San Diego, it cost us $900 to have the skid moved one hundred fifty feet to our booth space. The next trip, we used a different carrier, and they charged us as much as the first carrier, but the table arrived broken.

This will never work! I thought. The ideas and drawings for a new table started on the flight home.

Tables Number Three and Four

Essex began work almost as soon as we got back. The design this time was a lot more streamlined and constructed entirely out of aluminum. The LED lights on T2 created another slight problem. I really liked being able to change colors, but I had to take my hands off the table to turn the rheostats. It threw my timing off, and sometimes I even forgot. My brainiac son provided another brilliant solution. He suggested I use a digital projector mounted underneath the table that would change colors in time to the music. That was innovation number three.

To get the image large enough to fill the glass top, however, I had to attach the projector horizontally and use a mirror to reflect the light up to the glass. The mirror added one more breakable item to the case. SandStory T3 came out of the warehouse looking like a sleek, space-age coffee table. It only made one trip. At ninety-two pounds, it was still too heavy for the airlines to allow me to check it, and the metal frame broke the glass on the first flight. I even asked Essex to drill holes in it until it looked like a sleek, space-age coffee table—made of Swiss cheese. It only dropped the weight by about three pounds.

Back to the drawing board! Fortunately, the guys at Essex were quite patient, and although the cost of trying to get a table light enough, large enough, and easy enough to assemble was becoming exorbitant, they assured me they could figure it out. Three more weeks, and I got the call. Extruded aluminum with Allen-wrench joints assembled easily and it fit into a case that, although we would have to pay oversize fees, did weigh in at seventy-five pounds. The glass still looked vulnerable.

Back in my own garage/workshop, I took a hacksaw to the legs, reconfigured the brackets, built a holding tray for the glass, added two-inch foam to the inside of the case, and sewed straps to hold it all together. The goal was seventy pounds, to prevent overweight fees, but it was still oversize. With great trepidation, after all this work, I hefted it onto our bathroom scale. Seventy-one pounds. As we headed out for our next trip, I was hoping that our bathroom scale was off by one pound.

My love affair with Apple products goes back a long way. Although they are more expensive, the extra cost is offset by the tech support that covers both software and hardware. My apologies to the PC world, but Apple just always worked better for me. To get the lights to change colors, I created little iMovies on my Apple computer of the exact colors and shapes. The iMovie, loaded onto an iPod, synchronized the colors and music. It sure helped. T4 was ready to go, and it was not too long before, together, we earned Diamond status on Delta.

The Technical Shell Game

SandStory is an interesting blend of art and technology. It is a form of "ancient-future." Old-school, hand-manipulated images combined with high-tech video and sound. It is organic, using sand—a natural and very common material—and technological, using cameras, video projectors, and high-definition screens. Because I use my fingers and digital technology, it is digital-digital, if you get my meaning.

I have been doing artwork my entire life. I feel very comfortable with the drawing, which is easy to explain. Technology, on the other hand, is not my forte, and it changes about every three seconds. For that reason, I always send the technical specifications in a tech rider to the event planners. The message, however, does not always get through.

I have been forced to keep up with the very fast-changing world of technology, because I use a digital projector for my light source, driven by an iPod movie to change the colors, with a digital video camera overhead to capture the image and plug that into yet another digital projector. I have had to learn an entirely new language, not even mentioning the fact that each piece of equipment is made by a different manufacturer, and each has unique characteristics. All of these devices need to plug into each other and into the system provided by the venue where I perform.

The plugs come in a mind-numbing variety. Their acronyms, I am sure, stand for something. I do well to just remember the difference between an XLR, BNC, RCA, SUV, and BVD. If I don't have the right plug, or *jack*, as the techies call them, nothing works. Adding to the confusion is that every jack has a gender. Did you know that? "Male and female, He made them" and just like the Creator said, a marriage can only be between one male and one female. The result of all this is that I have to carry an entire bag full of adapters, some male, some female, quarter-inch, eighth-inch, two-prong, three-prong, red, yellow, white.

Wait, this gets even more fun. For the signal from my camera to get to the projector, which is provided by the venue, they have to speak the same language! Just like at the Tower of Babel, at some point in history, the signals were confounded. They all used to be analog, but then they became digital, and the one can no longer speak to the other.

Is it VGA? Is it composite or component? Perhaps HDMI? As soon as we cross the Atlantic Ocean, it becomes PAL instead of NTSC, and 110 volts of electrical current becomes 220. Do I have an adapter? Are 220 volts going to blow the circuits in my projector? Is all this confusion going to blow my mind?

Technology has definitely challenged me to do my homework. I used to break out in a cold sweat at the first technical hiccup. Now I just apologize, tell jokes, pull out my bag of adapters, start plugging jacks in and wiggling wires, with the hope of successful mating.

The beautiful old brick church in Greenville, South Carolina, was not ideal for a SandStory performance. Too many windows, too much light, a small projector and even smaller screen. Nonetheless, we persevered, set up our table, and handed our cable with a BNC jack, feeding a composite NTSC signal to the local tech guy. He looked at it as if it was Moses' staff turned into a snake and shook his head.

"This is all I've got," he said, holding up a cable with a VGA jack on the end of it. "It's for the computer that our youth director uses."

I asked him if he had been given a copy of the tech rider.

"Look," he said, "I volunteer on weekends. They don't tell me anything."

"Don't worry about it," I said, patting him on the shoulder. "We have never been to an event where we did not figure something out."

Finally, by using a TV cable borrowed from the nursery monitor and four or five of my adaptors, *presto*—we had the whole shebang working! It's always an adventure.

One of my favorites was a program we were doing for a college chapel service in a beautiful, high-tech auditorium. I was halfway through the "Passion of the Christ." The music was reverberating around the auditorium. I was so focused on what I was doing, the slight unrest in the audience didn't register. Out of the darkness, Cindy came tiptoeing up the aisle with an apologetic look and touched my shoulder. I jumped.

"The bulb in the projector burned out," she whispered. Someone had found her praying in a janitor's closet somewhere and sent her to come clue me in. I, of course, was so focused on the light table in front of me that everyone in the auditorium, bored at looking at a blank screen, could have gotten up and walked out without me noticing. I chatted and told jokes while a flustered student on the tech team scampered around and found an old projector in the library. We hooked it up quickly, and I finished the performance.

It is easy to get complacent. Just when I think I have a handle on the technology, that is when it's really dangerous. Technology is a moving target, a shell game. I think I know what is going on, and they change it on me. Now the tech people are asking for a new adaptor called HDSDI. I think that stands for "high dollars spent on digital interface."

As I type this, I am under the stage at the Mandalay Bay event center in Las Vegas, waiting to perform for a huge live event for about twenty thousand people. The producers designed a hydraulic lift so my table would rise out of the stage in a cloud of smoke. They also planned to project my sand images on a huge, seventy-foot digital LED screen. As I waited, suddenly the tech gurus appeared out of the darkness, hunched over, with their little digital flashlights. They interrupted to inform me they need to switch my camera over to HDSDI. *What the heck is that?*

Then, of course, there are the audio jacks. Don't even get me started with the quarter-inch, XLR, stereo, mono, or surround. It drives me bananas! Did you know—and I am not making this up— audio guys in the past used to use jacks called "banana clips."

CHAPTER FOUR

FIRST GIGS

Large Corporations and Little Churches

Don't despise the day of small things …
—Psalm 145:7

My Beret and First DVD

God bless him, Dr. Joe McClaren did not give up on us. A year after his first request, he called again asking us to come perform "The Passion" SandStory for his Easter service.

"Bring lots of product. Our people love to support your ministry," he said on the phone.

We didn't have any "product." I had run off a few DVD copies of my attic-filming experience but had given most of them away. I set up my light table in my studio at home and filmed it again. It was much better this time; practice does pay off. As I was reviewing my amateur filming efforts, I noticed a glare on the top of my head as the few strands of hair I had left poked into the screen from time to time. It looked hideous, like a hovering alien spaceship with tentacles.

My son came to the rescue again. He not only skates on the razor edge of technology but fashion as well. For my birthday, he gave me a sporty, black driving hat, recommending I wear it backward to look cool. I'm not sure how cool I looked, but it kept the feelers on the alien spaceship from invading the film, and it worked perfectly. I refilmed so we could have some "product" for Joe's church.

Ordering five hundred DVDs seemed outrageous. We would, no doubt, have them stacked in our garage for the next decade and have to give them away as gifts to all our relatives, friends, neighbors, the mailman, and any strangers who happened to stop by for directions.

Carillon United Methodist Church

Three performances on Sunday morning all ended in standing ovations that left me feeling overwhelmed with joy and awe. Cindy and I were also treated with such kindness that we glowed with appreciation. What also surprised us was that the one hundred DVDs we had packed in our suitcase were gone by the second service. They cleaned us out.

The greatest kindnesses came from a Hispanic family who met us at the service. After a warm embrace, we spoke together in Spanish, my native language, and shared our common heritage. The old father pointed to my hat and said, *"Mira, José, el sombrero tiene que ser una boina de España."* (If you are going to wear a hat, it needs to be a Spanish beret.)

Ten days later, a package arrived in the mail containing an authentic beret from the famous Tupida Tolosa Hat Company in Madrid, Spain. I have worn a beret for every performance since.

Intercontinental Hotel

I really thought we had hit the big time when I received a call from the Intercontinental Hotel in Milwaukee, Wisconsin. They wanted us to perform at the grand opening of their newest hotel. In all of the excitement, God has a way of keeping me humble. I showed up at this fancy-dancy place, only to discover that we were performing not on a stage but right in the middle of the lobby, with milling hordes of folks there to celebrate the opening.

My SandStory drawings were not to be projected on a giant thirty-foot screen but on TV screens scattered throughout the hotel. The vast majority of guests would never know I was there, much less that I was performing it live. By the time I got started, people were crammed in tighter than on a Japanese subway. On their way through the lobby, revelers often set their empty glasses on my table. Confused about what I was doing, some would start playing in the sand. A kitty scratching in his litter box would have gotten more attention. It was a dismal experience. I've been reminded of this on quite a few occasions: "Pride goes before a fall." Don't get too stuck on your own importance, dude! It is not about you.

Lexmark

An invitation to perform for Lexmark International in Lexington, Kentucky, reminded me again of the importance of a good story. It began as a challenge. Our home church had invited us to do a segment for a Christmas program that was very well received. After the program, an event planner for Lexmark approached me about performing for their "Diversity Day."

Christ admonished us to love everybody. I wanted to tell that story in a secular setting. What resulted was a very sweet piece I called "Friends." It portrayed the importance of getting along with everyone. I have performed it dozens of times since.

White Oak Pond Church

Friends are the ones who will let you perform, even when they don't have a clue what you do. Just down the street from where we lived in Richmond, Kentucky, is a little country church that was founded in 1790 and whose congregation has been meeting regularly ever since. It was, at one point, outside of town, but the town has grown and enfolded it. Most of the parishioners have been attending since the doors opened (well, almost), and Reverend Rusty Rechenbach had been their pastor for twenty-five years.

One of the younger attendees had seen us perform and passed our information on to Rusty. On the phone, I tried to explain SandStory. They did have a projector in the children's room, but the sanctuary did not have a screen. Large stained-glass windows ran the length of the ancient chapel. Undeterred, Rusty wanted us to come badly enough that he hand-built shutters for the lovely glass artwork, borrowed a screen, and hung it over the communion table in the chancel.

That Sunday morning, after heavy promotion of the event, the pews were crammed full. Rusty announced me as if I were one of the original apostles, and off I went. After it was over, the comment I heard most was, "I have never seen the young people sit so quietly for so long."

The highlight of the day was a question from a very elderly gentleman who asked to have his wheelchair pushed up to my SandStory table. He peered through glasses that looked like antique hand-blown glass paperweights. "You draw pitchers here'n the sand?" I nodded and demonstrated, running my hand through the sand. The old guy squinted up at the screen. "How'dja git the pitchers up thar?"

Diana United Methodist Church

The Methodist Church, I discovered, has at least one congregation in every zip code in the nation. With about nine million adherents, you can find them everywhere. Most of those churches have fewer than one hundred members.

Cindy and I traveled back in time to the rural community of Diana, Tennessee. There we enjoyed a log cabin, a horse-drawn-buggy ride, country food, and the hospitality of Diana United Methodist Church. Three ArtStory drawings and a SandStory presentation made the three days exciting, and the friendly people of Diana made it memorable.

If you really want to slow down, experience a different era, and reconnect, make reservations for a couple of nights at the Lairdland

Farm B&B. Join the wonderful folks at Diana UMC for church on Sunday morning. Get Doug Wolaver to give you a ride in his buggy. I guarantee that you will experience life as it was a hundred years ago.

About forty people dotted the hundred-seat auditorium Sunday morning. Word got around after the service that some guy was doing "pretty cool drawings" at the Diana church. By Sunday night, the crowd swelled to eighty. On Monday evening, the auditorium was full. Tuesday, our last night, I performed my only SandStory piece. It exploded into a family-night free-for-all with standing room only, just like an old-time revival.

Crystal Cove Community Church

Another church popped up on the radar that summer. It was small, but for a different reason than Diana: Crystal Cove was quite new. Founded by good friends from college, Phil and Sue Engleman and a few of their friends, it was part of a wave of churches crafted to reach a new generation. A casual atmosphere, with coffee and bagels before the service and contemporary music, gave it a "Starbucks" feel. High-tech SandStory fit right in. They asked us to perform Sunday morning and Sunday night, exhausting my entire repertoire. I felt like a one-man band that only knew four songs. It was obvious I needed to create more new SandStories.

Yellow River Baptist Church

Buzz and Kathy Nofal also fall into the category of "old friends." I am not saying that they are old (which they are), but that we have known them for a long, long time. They had heard of our leap of faith into this wild and crazy new career. For a time, they also had an itinerant ministry, traveling and speaking in churches. Buzz hilariously described it as his dog-and-pony show: arriving, setting up, performing, selling merchandise, packing up, and moving on. We laughed so hard at his description that we had tears in our eyes. It was a reminder that much like the early circuit-riding preachers, our time with people was limited, and we often moved on without hearing if anything we had done had left any long-term impact at all.

Yellow River Baptist Church was a relatively small audience compared to the huge venues we would perform in later. At this church, Cindy began to pray that we could have an impact that would remain. After the performance, people said things that encouraged me to believe that in a spiritual way, they would remember God had moved in their lives.

An elderly man came up to me and said, "Joe, when I was six years old, an artist came to our church and told a story and drew a picture using chalks. It has been almost seventy years, but I can remember that service to this day."

Similar comments pop up almost every time I perform. When they say something like that, Cindy and I wonder if seventy years from now, somebody might remember the wacky SandStory artist who came to their church and the impact he made. The answer lay in something we both already knew, but Cindy really made it work.

CHAPTER FIVE

THE REAL POWER

What Does Prayer Have to Do with Anything?

In all your prayers, ask God for what you need.
—*Philippians 4:6*

*C*indy has been my companion throughout this entire amazing trip. She has followed me from Kentucky to the ends of the Earth and back. She handled strange countries, unusual venues, and hyper-stressed-out clients, mostly with great calm. Being in the auditorium while I perform made Cindy anxious. Potential technical glitches, the size of the audience, new and difficult stories, none of which she could control, all added to her anxiety.

The National Youth Workers Convention took it all to a new level. I was nervous, Cindy even more so. She decided not to stay in the performance at all, committing herself to finding a quiet room in which to pray. It was here that the value of the ministry of prayer really began to shine. Not only was this a huge crowd, but it was the first time we had performed for a conference at which dozens of very well-known musicians, speakers, and entertainers were featured. My ten-minute SandStory performance was scheduled right at the very beginning. I was concerned it would get lost in the flood of other performers.

After helping me get set up and ready, Cindy slipped out, found a quiet spot, and prayed. I came off the stage vibrating like a tuning fork. I know that her prayers gave my performance a power that stood out, despite my nervousness.

Specific prayer is always more effective than general prayer. During one of the NYWC performances, Cindy specifically prayed that God would change someone's life. Later she told me that a giant, head-shaved, tattooed, biker-looking dude approached her, put both fists on the table, leaned well within her personal space, and with tears running down his face said, "That touched me in a way that has changed me forever."

As our ministry progressed, her prayers have become more specific, and God has answered in specific ways. Cindy likes to find her "prayer room" where she can hear my music. She always knows what story I am performing and prays for each image.

At a pastors' conference in Dallas, Texas, I was only given ten minutes to tell a SandStory. That was the perfect length for "The Prodigal Son." It ends with the father embracing the son, which I then change into the Good Shepherd holding the lost lamb. It really is my favorite SandStory.

Cindy told me later that evening that she specifically prayed that the pastors would feel God's embrace. Very shortly after my performance, a teary-eyed pastor approached Cindy at our table and said, "Please tell Joe that I have never felt like that before. I felt that God was holding me in His arms." I get goose bumps again, even as I type this. That exact thing happens on a regular basis.

I often hear discussions about the efficacy of prayer. It is natural for the skeptic to wonder if it really does any good. Cindy often prays that people watching the SandStories will be impacted, regardless of where they are. At the Palazzo Theater in Las Vegas, an elderly, weathered man with worn, homespun clothing that did not look like it came from Brooks Brothers—or even Wal-Mart, for that matter—waited a long time to see me. His face was a deeply tanned mass of wrinkles, brightened by two twinkling black eyes. He stepped up to me and took my hands in his gnarled, leathery ones. Very deliberately, he turned my hands over and looked down at them. His clear eyes then met mine, and he spoke in broken English.

"I am from Armenia. I come here to see you. I know you draw pictures of Jesus."

At that point, I began weeping, reached out my arms, and embraced him. With dozens of onlookers still milling around, he haltingly told me a little of his story. He was a Christian from a small town and an even smaller church near Yerevan, Armenia. Somehow, he had seen the Prodigal Son SandStory, including the image of Christ holding a small lamb. Although he had never been to the United States, he had relatives in Las Vegas and determined to come see the show. We embraced again, and as he pulled away he said, "We … my church … pray for you."

How humbling to think that people, literally halfway around the globe, were touched by my SandStory and traveled to Las Vegas to pray for me.

I discovered another component to the power of prayer. Pastors, missionaries, friends, and random Christians let us know in person and on Facebook that they were praying for us and for SandStory. Thanks to all of you who have prayed for this rather unusual ministry. I began asking some of these faithful people to pray for specific things. Invariably, if I am paying attention, the answers surface somewhere, at some event.

My latest prayer request is for the young, artistic people who shyly sidle up to my table after most of the crowd has cleared out. I can usually recognize them by the way they dress or the sketch pad under their arm. They are the artists, writers, poets, musicians, and creative kids who are trying desperately to find their voice, their stage, their ministry, or a place to be heard. As much as I can, I take the time to look through their sketches, read their poems or stories, and pray with them. I am beginning to hear from these young people about successes with their artwork and the encouragement they have felt. If you are one of our faithful prayer supporters, please add these young artists to your list. Prayers like this take a long time to produce fruit.

Invariably, when I am backstage, my phone will sound a soft *ding*, indicating the arrival of a text message from Cindy: "I am praying for you." When Cindy prays, I feel calmness wash over me, and I am deeply moved by what I hear people say. Lives are changed when people pray.

CHAPTER SIX

MAKING IT BIG

Our Big Break and New Challenges

You are behind me and already ahead of me.
—Psalm 139:5

I tell people that I do have a claim to fame. My nephew, Jeremy Bush, aka "B-Wack," was the drummer for The David Crowder Band. If you have not heard of them, I can tell you that at one time, they were unquestionably one of the top Christian worship bands in the world. I say *world* because they have, in fact, traveled the globe performing their wonderful music. Today he plays for the dynamic Christian group "Digital Age."

When I took the plunge and decided I was going to try to make a living as a SandStory performer, thinking of ways to promote myself came as a natural consequence of my years in advertising. *If I could do a SandStory along with The David Crowder Band, that could get me some real exposure,* I thought. But God is behind us and already ahead of us in every endeavor.

I sent Jeremy a copy of that first "Passion" DVD, with the hopes of doing something live with his band. He told me that he was going to pass it on to a friend at the National Youth Workers Convention. Now, again, for those of you not in the know, the NYWC is the premier event for youth workers around the country, put on by Youth Specialties. Jeremy passed my DVD along to Tic Long, the head honcho at YS, with the promise that they would watch it.

A Fateful Moment

Tic later described the story to me. Youth Specialties gets crates and crates of music and entertainment videos from those hoping to get on the main stage for these huge events. When my nephew, Jeremy, handed my DVD to Tic, he said with his typical quiet, earnest voice, "You really need to watch this, Tic, because it is my uncle Joe. You are going to watch it, aren't you?"

Tic walked into his staff meeting, where they were planning the next NYWC. He tossed my DVD on the table and said, "Sorry, guys, we need to watch a bit of this, because B-Wack gave it to me, and I *know* he will ask me if we did." They watched more than just a bit, and all agreed to give me a shot. For me, it was a *huge* shot! Three venues: San Diego, St. Louis, and Atlanta, with a total of approximately fifteen thousand attendees.

Knight on a White Horse

Somebody had a clue what I was in for, but it wasn't me. The onslaught of booking requests, schedule juggling, and negotiations that were going to land in my lap was totally outside my realm of experience. Tim Grable didn't look like a knight. There was no white horse. In fact, Tim sort of shuffled into my life in Denver, Colorado, almost a year before I took the main stage at NYWC. He looked a little nerdy, with a goofy smile on his face. He asked me what I did and handed me a card stating that he had a booking agency.

Cindy and I were still working at Whitestone Country Inn, but we were very seriously considering launching out on our own. Tim asked me to send him some material. He didn't know what I did, so I put one of my attic-filmed DVDs in a folder with a description of what SandStory was. Nothing happened. Nothing, for almost a year. When Tim got word that we were going to be on the main stage at NYWC, he knew it would change my life.

A couple of months before the event, Tim called. We talked and talked and talked. Then I talked with Cindy. He sounded very sensible. It didn't really matter much to me; I was going to have an agent! I had never had an agent before, and it sounded very cool. What I didn't know about this nice, geeky guy was that he had been booking people at NYWC and venues all over the world for almost twenty years. He was one of the top handlers of Christian performers in the United States. He was a pro!

Since then, I have been amazed at what he has done. Tim has opened doors, negotiated events, smoothed out the bumps, and been the crucial factor in moving us from the sandlot to the big leagues. Tim, a million thanks!

Serious Jitters

I was pretty cavalier about not being nervous in front of an audience. That was a "normal" audience, a group of people that you could count. When I walked into the massive convention center in San Diego with seats for five thousand youth workers, chairs that extended almost as far as the eye could see, my knees felt a little weak.

The main stage had a screen that was thirty feet high and seventy feet long, not to mention seven or eight other screens suspended from the ceiling around the convention hall. When we started doing a video check, my hands appeared on the screens at least twelve feet high. Every little tremor was magnified a thousand times.

They had scheduled me right at the beginning, the very first person on stage. Not only that, but Tic had talked me into doing a new SandStory piece on Creation. Whew! The pressure was really on. They opened the doors, and the audience poured in like Noah's flood, all trying to get the best seats. From my vantage point, standing beside the stage, there was not an empty seat in the hall. Sweat started running down my back. The timer clock ticked the seconds. The lights dimmed. I heard my cue. I was on! Just like Tim had promised, it changed my life.

Before my performance at the NYWC was even over, folks were striding toward our merchandise table with the determined look of "book that guy" in their eyes. The phone was ringing. Requests were pouring in and I was suddenly in huge demand. One of the many bookings that came out of that performance was for Baytown, Texas. Jack Hall, the worship director at Second Baptist Church, wanted us to perform for their Christmas program. That was not a problem. The problem was that he wanted original, customized pieces that went with the lyrics of their live music.

"Sure," I glibly told Tim. "We can try anything." Actually, I didn't have any idea how to do it. One of their songs was cute and funny, one serious, and one sweet and touching. To be able to pull it off, I knew having a studio at home was essential. After setting up my spare table, I locked myself in, put the music on repeat, and started creating these new stories, practicing them over and over again.

One of the problems that plagued me was the issue of control. Almost all of my artwork "B.S." (before sand) was done with pen and ink. Fine lines and very detailed artwork gave me almost total control. Sand, on the other hand, has a personality of its own. When you toss it or dribble it or run your fingers through it, the results are *never* exactly the same twice.

Working in sand is like playing an instrument. Like a cello or violin without any frets, each note has to be practiced over and over until the pitch is perfect. As I practiced and improved my technique, much of what happened was a repetition of what I had done many times before. Then I discovered improvisation.

Way back, in the days when I played the clarinet, jazz music was at the top of my list. The improvised music that came out of Dixieland was the best of the best. It was fluid, natural, and often produced melodies neither the audience nor the musician expected. Just like jazz, the resulting SandStory images are always a little different.

Improvisation was a new direction, and if I could get past the jitters, I loved it.

The biggest element in becoming comfortable with my SandStory illustrations was trusting God. I would practice and practice until I had a real lock on the hand movements, but even if the swipe was exactly like I had done it a hundred times before, the sand would not always cooperate. That is when I began letting God have the final control. I would do all I could, and then, when the moment came to step onto the stage, I would prayerfully say, "Okay, God, it is all You from here on."

After many hours of practice, a good bit of nervousness, and a leap of faith, the Christmas event at Baytown Second Baptist was a great success. Since then, custom work has become a huge part of my SandStory performances. Although challenging, my work has become much more versatile and unique.

Swiss Army Knife Performer

With the willingness to be flexible, I had the opportunity to include my early ArtStory drawings like "The Face of Christ." I developed more than a dozen line drawings with stories woven into the details. My life experience gave me stories to tell. Many of the event planners asked me to be the keynote speaker, include an ArtStory drawing or two, and then toss the SandStory on top like the proverbial cherry on the ice-cream sundae. It is more fun than anything I have ever done.

One of the real surprises in this wild adventure was the huge variety of churches and denominations that invited me to come and perform. Just in the month of March of our first year, I performed at events from seven different denominations: Methodists, Baptists, Lutherans, Episcopalians, Church of Christ, Catholics, and several nondenominational churches. They all seemed to enjoy the SandStory performances.

What I should have realized very early in my use of the arts was the fact that people, regardless of their religion, gender, or ethnic background, all appreciate art. Not all the same medium or genre, but the right music, movies, videos, paintings, or performance will eventually "sneak past the watchful dragons" and touch the most hardened person's soul. I know it to be true, yet on occasion, the impact of art sneaks up and surprises me.

Chapelwood United Methodist Church

The women's retreat sponsored by Chapelwood UMC in Houston, Texas, was one of those surprises. About a hundred women from an affluent, fairly conservative church met at a retreat center for a weekend of encouragement and worship. A stately, poised, white-haired matron with perfect Southern diction was the moderator and keynote speaker. They invited me to be the culture segment of the event. I was the token male as well. At the end of my performance, I expected a polite smattering of applause. In stunned silence, with tears ruining the perfect mascara and streaking the expensive makeup, the ladies enthusiastically expressed their genuine appreciation. Many of them said I was the highlight of the event.

Detroit Diocese of Catholic Men

I know that the word *surprise* shows up often in this story, but God is still surprising me at every turn. Tim, my veteran booking guy, called with this next event, an invitation to perform at a men's retreat in Michigan. It was supposed to attract five thousand Catholic men. This was new to me.

"The Archdiocese of Detroit wants you to be the closing performance for their event," Tim announced.

"Fine, we are in," I answered.

I expected the traditional, rather stuffy church I was familiar with as a boy. The Catholic church I knew growing up in Mexico City, Mexico, had services in Latin; it was filled with rituals, saints, and icons and did not encourage participation or lay involvement.

The flavor of this conference was very different. The Catholic men had gathered to worship Christ, learn the Scriptures, sing contemporary worship songs, and hear from none other than prison fellowship director Tom Pratt. I was surrounded by these men excited about glorifying God and lifting up Jesus Christ. It was an invigorating experience.

Over the years, I have discovered genuine spiritual life in many of the multitude of denominations for which I have performed. Finding out what produces it has been of great interest to me. First there is a love for Christ, followed closely by a hunger to know the Scriptures. An enthusiasm for an upright life and a close fellowship with others of the faith produces a desire to share it. As I get to know these people of faith, I have experienced that unexplainable communion of the spirit that identifies another person as a member of the same spiritual family.

It has astounded me how much of that genuine faith is out there. I am convinced, just as God had to convince Elisha, who when feeling sorry for himself and believing he was the only true follower left, discovered that there were yet five thousand who had not succumbed to following the pagan god Baal. Cindy and I have met genuine, Christ-following believers in most of the places we go. And yes, we have even discovered real, twice-born, Spirit-filled, water-baptized, wholly consecrated, Scripture-quoting, God-fearing, gospel-sharing, Christians in—insert your church or denomination here.

CHAPTER SEVEN

THE FRIENDS, THE FAITHFUL, AND THE FAMOUS

Owed and Awed

Do you see a man skilled in his work? He will stand before Kings.
—Proverbs 22:29

Our Friends

*O*ver and over again, I have been profoundly grateful to those who not only invited me to perform but then were willing to invite us back again … and again. Tic Long of YS invited us to perform at NYWC the following year in San Diego, Nashville, and Pittsburgh. Those events have been huge in giving me more exposure and generating more bookings. I have also made friends with many youth directors, pastors, and church leaders who contacted Tim and invited me to perform at their conferences and churches. One of the unused tools in my Swiss Army knife of experiences was doing the cartoon sketches of people who came by our booth. As they sat for the two-minute sketches, I had time to get their names and hear a little of their stories. I still remember those people.

My son, José, also pops back into the story with the great idea to call what I was doing "SandStory." He even came up with the slogan that I have used ever since: *"Epic stories in a New Light."* It sounded a little presumptuous to me at first, but the truth was that in my feeble way, what I was trying to depict in sand were truly "epic" stories.

Tim Grable, my faithful agent, has stuck with me through irascible clients, confusing languages, complex negotiations, and technical complications. He has gotten me into—and out of—the most amazing places and negotiated deals that were way beyond my ability to work out, not to mention that neither Cindy nor I had the time. My heart always beats a little faster when the phone rings and Tim's name appears on the caller ID.

His comments almost invariably start with, "Hello, Joe, I have been going back and forth with these folks in Libya, Morocco, Egypt, Hong Kong, Beirut, Brazil, Italy ..." or some other far-flung place. Or it might be, "Joe, I have been talking with the BBC, NBC, the Saudi government, or *America's Got Talent.*" (More on that later.) All those places and people actually called and wanted me to perform.

The other great affirmation was the continued invitations to the Asbury Seminary Presidents' retreat. Cindy and I got to be a part of three events in Marco Island, Florida, two at the Broadmoor in Colorado Springs, Colorado, and one at The Cove in North Carolina. Each time, we were well received and treated royally. For their ninetieth anniversary, I was invited to perform a custom piece about the ministry of Francis Asbury and the founding of Asbury Seminary. As an alumnus, it was always a pleasure to share some of our adventures with the wonderful people there. We continue to be invited back.

The Faithful

When you don't travel much or only travel for business or vacation, it is very easy to see only the chaos in the world through the very narrow, filtered reports that appear on a TV screen. It can be very discouraging. Very little of lasting spiritual impact seems to be going on. "I am the only one left," moaned Elijah. "Take heart! God has not forgotten us, nor does he sleep," he is reminded.

The most encouraging aspect of what Cindy and I do is the thrill of landing in a city we have never been to before and being picked up at the airport by a Christian bubbling over with God's love. We are transported to some building or church, to find hundreds, and in many cases thousands, of eager believers thronging together to worship, praise God, and then go out to reach the world with His grace. They are active, sharing their faith, caring for the poor, the sick, and the afflicted. They regularly visit prisons, hospitals, and rest homes. Many are busy rebuilding houses ravaged by tornadoes, hurricanes, and earthquakes. They are givers, taking up offerings for orphans, prisoners, refugees, and victims of catastrophes in all those devastated places we see on TV. They seldom make the news, but they sure do make a difference.

Winterfest in Gatlinburg, Tennessee, attracted more than thirteen thousand young people between the ages of twelve and eighteen. Polite, cheerful kids in those dreaded teen years sat for hours, listening to stories of sacrifice and commitment told by missionaries who had returned from some very desolate places. The young people then packed tens of thousands of protein-rich, ready-to-cook meals to ship to refugee camps. They collected thousands of dollars for relief efforts and sponsored hundreds of orphans from the poorest countries around the world. Amazing!

Beaver Dam, Kentucky, is not much on the map. It is so small, it probably has a ZIP code with a decimal point. But in this little town, one of the churches has been pulling in over a thousand high school students annually for a weeklong event that involves working on projects like Habitat for Humanity, visiting nursing homes, cleaning up neighborhood parks, and delivering meals to shut-ins.

With all the criticism of failing educational institutions, I was thrilled to perform at an event at a school in San Juan Capistrano, California. Almost the entire school attended a voluntary spirit day, where the excited students dedicated themselves to vocations of service.

In another part of the country, twenty-five thousand—you read it right—twenty-five thousand teenagers packed into the Thompson-Boling Arena in Knoxville, Tennessee. They cheered enthusiastically during a biblical message about morals, purity, and values. You won't read about it in the newspaper or hear it on the evening news, but it happened. I know. I performed there, and I saw it with my own eyes.

Big churches, small churches, conferences, conventions, and seminars all over the United States and the world are getting together to affirm, encourage, and lift up the name of God. It also has been a great encouragement that the particular denomination made no difference. I have performed for an estimated thirty-five different church affiliations and many more "flavors" than that—conservative, contemporary, blended, cutting-edge, and traditional. With very few exceptions, I found them to be enthused, hungry, and energized to build, promote, and reach out for the kingdom of God.

Having spent almost sixty years as a member, youth pastor, worship leader, teacher, and pastor in many different churches, I know the difference between a "live" church and a "dead" one. It seems as if the churches that have the courage to try something as different as SandStory already have the courage to believe the Bible, trust God, and move forward. Hallelujah!

The Famous

Performing for corporate events was no longer new, but I was surprised to get the opportunity to perform for all the top executives, dealership owners, and Chinese dignitaries at a conference for Mercedes-Benz in Beijing, China. It was one of only a handful of trips that I took without my sensible, organized, on-time manager/wife/friend, Cindy. The trip almost didn't happen because she was not along to keep me on track.

I was scheduled to leave Lexington for Boulder, Colorado, for a performance before going on to Los Angeles, California, to catch the flight to Beijing. In Boulder, I discovered my passport was missing. I started frantic phone calls, trying to locate it at three in the morning. Finally, a very gracious ticket agent found the lost passport, popped it in a Delta Dash packet, and put it on the next plane to LA. With minutes to spare, I picked up the packet in the Delta mailroom, ran to the plane, and was the last passenger to board. Cindy would have checked and made sure I had my passport.

I still cannot explain SandStory to someone who has never seen a performance. I select powerful, emotional music and then tell a story with the images and choreograph my hand movements to weave the story, music, and images into a powerful experience. It is organic, emotional, and visceral all at once. People are moved to tears, cheers, and standing ovations. Even a corporate logo can bring an audience to their feet cheering. A big part of the magic is the mystery of getting caught up in what image is going to appear next. That magic captivated the Mercedes-Benz executives in Beijing.

Some countries in the Middle East became interested in my work because, face it, they have a *lot* of sand over there. My first gig for the Arabs was for the Bank of Dubai. It was a very interesting banquet. All the men, dressed in white, sat on one side and ignored all the women, dressed in black, on the other. There were different buffet lines and no interaction between the two groups. I told the SandStory of banking in the Middle East. Deserts and camels became a city growing out of the sand. The camels transformed into luxury vehicles, and the bedouins become sheiks.

I felt it was not my most moving performance, but they got as excited as I have ever seen bankers get. The Arabs seemed to like the SandStories enough to invite me back a number of times.

In Saudi Arabia, I performed for King Mohammad Saudi Al Maktoum, to celebrate the grand opening of the new King Abdullah University of Science and Technology (KAUST). Someone from the campus had attended our event in Dubai and contacted my agent, Tim. They invited me to create a custom SandStory describing the explosive construction of this fabulous, state-of-the-art facility, completed in one thousand days. I was asked to perform it for the new students, the staff, and the king himself. He had endowed the university with $10 billion US dollars. That's *billion* with a capital B.

At one point, it was the largest construction project on the planet. Forty-eight thousand men per shift, working three eight-hour shifts, completed the most modern, lavish college campus ever. The king's followers managed to pull off this near-impossible feat with thousands of workers from India, Bangladesh, and the Philippines sweeping, cleaning, and putting the finishing touches on the beautiful campus for the grand opening. Telling the story in sand made perfect sense, since the entire campus had risen out of the empty dunes on the edge of the Red Sea.

The night of the event generated its own level of excitement. We had to vacate the tent three times so bomb-sniffing dogs could go through the venue. Metal detectors and luggage checks were required because of the king's attendance. Cindy almost had her camera confiscated by a very adamant, Kalashnikov-toting guard who kept shouting, "No peektures, no peektures."

I started, very appropriately, with sand dunes, camels, and date palms overlooking the Red Sea. Then the buildings of KAUST began rising out of the desert, crouded with students and professors. The final image was my SandStory drawing of King Abdullah holding the KAUST logo in his hand. The audience cheered when I did the "peekture" of the king.

After the performance, some of the women in attendance were bold enough to step up to my sand table and admit they wept when I drew the final image of their beloved king. If you want a unique educational experience, send in your application to KAUST. The trip alone is worth it.

Almost two years after the KAUST event, I was given another opportunity to tell SandStories in Saudi Arabia. The annual trip to Mecca that all Muslims are required to take is called the Hajj. It usually falls sometime in November. Millions of the faithful from around the world make the trek to Mecca.

The government has established the Ministry of Hajj to help the pilgrims arrive and depart safely. They recruit volunteers who coordinate logistics, transportation, food, security, and a host of other details. When the sand all settles, and the pilgrims return home, the ministry gives a lavish banquet for the volunteers as a special thank-you for their service.

Dr. Bandar bin Mohammed bin Hamza Asaad Al-Hajjar, minister of the Hajj, invited me to come to Jeddah to tell the SandStory of the Hajj for the volunteers. I had met the minister at the KAUST grand opening. The e-mail conversations, selection of music, and detailed information involved a lengthy process, during which I learned a great deal of Muslim history, including some words in Arabic. It took a long time to get ready for that event.

On the day of the banquet at the Jeddah Hilton Hotel, Cindy and I were the only Westerners in the entire place. The men were dressed all in white robes with white *kufi*, or turbans. The women wore black, many covered entirely with the full, black shift or *habib*, nothing showing except their eyes. Cindy had been given one and instructed to wear it, but the habib was as big as a large Arab tent. She opted for a floor-length dress and a black head scarf.

The women were segregated in a separate room and had to watch the proceedings on a large screen. An interesting side note revealed to me by my spy in the women's enclave was that as soon as they got behind closed doors, the habibs came off, and under the modest, drab, black covering was the most astonishing array of banquet gowns, high-fashion, high-heeled footwear, low-cut necklines, and bling she had ever seen.

I, on the other hand, was invited to sit at the head table with Dr. Bandar, who reclined on a real, red-velvet, gold-leaf throne. By watching and following all of those at my table carefully, I managed to get through the banquet without doing anything egregiously ill-mannered or creating an international incident.

Then it was my turn. When they introduced me, they pronounced my name quite accurately. It was the only thing I understood. Undoubtedly, the story was very meaningful for all those in attendance, and the men at least—I couldn't see the women—gave me a standing ovation. Later, in excellent English, Dr. Bandar proclaimed it was the best Hajj banquet he had ever attended.

I was invited to yet another banquet scheduled by the Saudis, only this time it was in Boston. Alwaleed Bin Talal al Saud handles the investments for the Saud family of Saudi Arabia. Reportedly one of the richest men in the world, he owns three palaces and the really cool yacht used in the James Bond movie, *"Thunderball."* One of his charities invited President Jimmy Carter and other American and Arab dignitaries to dine and talk about religious tolerance at a hotel in Boston.

This SandStory was about how we should love each other, regardless of our differences. It was a very sweet piece, showing two young girls from different backgrounds becoming friends. The crowd, which was a diverse mixture of cultures and nationalities, was lavish in their response. After it was all over, I chatted with Alwaleed, and he introduced me to his incredibly attractive young wife, Princess Ameera. I guess if you have the palaces *and* the yacht, you get the lovely girl too. Beautiful and intelligent, she spoke perfect English and was very serious about finding common ground between Arabs and Americans.

The next year, Jennifer Lopez and her ex, Marc Anthony, teamed up to put on a reality TV show called *Q'Viva!*, similar to *America's Got Talent.* Marc Anthony, Latin-American salsa idol, and J-Lo traveled to South America looking for undiscovered talent. They produced a competition show with the best Latin-American performers. From the best singers, dancers, and musicians, they selected their favorites during an eight-week series.

Q'Viva! concluded with a live concert in the Mandalay Bay Convention Center in Las Vegas for thousands of adoring fans. Marc Anthony had seen my work on YouTube and demanded that I be part of the show, even if I had not been discovered in a *barrio* in the slums of Mexico.

Jennifer Lopez and Marc Anthony's fans had never heard of Joe Castillo, the SandStory artist. J-Lo sang her opening number right before I came on, and I performed with Marc Anthony's tear-jerking song, *"¿Que Es Patria?"* ("What Is Homeland?") Latinos are very, very emotional and expressive. As I came off the stage, one exuberant woman reached over the balcony, grabbed my hands, and began kissing them as she said, *"¡Que manos tan benditas!"* (What blessed hands!) I got a standing ovation. I can't remember if either Jen or Marc got one.

That event was followed by my stint on *America's Got Talent*. There I got to rub elbows with Nick Cannon, Howard Stern, Sharon Osbourne, and Howie Mandel. Most of my contact with people at this level was brief and the conversations relatively trivial. What I realized was that all these celebrities, regardless of their status, fame, or money, were people just like us. When we talked, it didn't take long to discover that they all had their own special struggles and problems. What I prayed often was that perhaps something of what God had placed in me by His spirit would have an impact on them, and a seed would be planted for someone else to water. I knew that God cared about them all.

CHAPTER EIGHT

ADVENTURES

Crazy Things Happen on the Road

When the flood comes, it will not overwhelm you.
—Psalm 139:5

Dubai, United Arab Emirates

*T*he event for the Dubai Bank began with twenty-four hours on three flights from Chicago to Atlanta to Paris to Dubai. It left us feeling much like runway roadkill. We deplaned at 1:00 a.m. Dubai time. They did their best to take care of us. An airport concierge service provided us with a young woman decked out in a pretty, gold-embroidered shift, black slacks, and gold slippers—obviously not from Dubai. She introduced herself as Joy and guided us to a comfortable lounge, where we were given tea and cookies while she went to collect our luggage.

Bad news: our luggage didn't show. My light table and all the electronics were still in Atlanta. I started getting frantic. Cindy started praying. The next flight from Atlanta did not arrive until *after* the event. Joy was sweet and apologetic. After almost two futile hours of trying to get our luggage to Dubai, Joy led us out to our hotel limo in the blistering nighttime 115-degree heat. An overeager baggage handler, pushing a cart loaded with luggage, rammed Cindy from behind, and she almost fell. The combination of exhaustion, frustration over lost luggage, and the pressure of having to tell the event producer who flew us all the way to Dubai that we would not be able to perform, was too much. Cindy burst into tears. Joy, who had been watching us closely, made reassuring sounds and then turned and asked me directly, "Mr. Joe, you are Christian? I see your website. You work as pastor?"

Shocked at her question, I nodded. "Yes, we are Christians."

She smiled a big smile and then said something I would never have expected to hear in the Arab emirate of Dubai: "May I pray for you?"

I agreed, of course, thinking that she would quietly whisper a prayer for us when she got home or found a quiet moment. Not so. We were standing at the traveler pickup of the huge Dubai airport, surrounded by hundreds of Arabs in full garb. Joy laid her hand softly on Cindy's shoulder and began to pray. "Lord Jesus, please give Mr. Joe and Mrs. Cindy strength. I ask that you bring Mr. Joe's table and give him great success."

Joy became our angel. She was a calm presence at a frustrating time. We discovered later that she and ten other young Christians from the Philippines had moved to Dubai and found jobs specifically to share the love of Christ in a place with very little light. Their little evangelistic "church" met in one of their cramped apartments, prayed, encouraged each other, and then went out to various jobs to plant seeds and spread the love of Christ.

Joy's prayers were answered. The producer of the event called in a carpenter, who built a light table to my specifications in three hours. I went out to the beach at the convention resort where we were staying, to collect about two pounds of sand. With a borrowed colander from the kitchen, I sifted out the large pieces, and the show went on.

Joy is still one of our Facebook friends, and we continue to follow her missionary adventures in Dubai. Two weeks ago, we heard of her engagement to one of her fellow missionaries.

Jeddah, Saudi Arabia

Only a few months later, Cindy and I found ourselves in the middle of something right out of the pages of the latest Joel Rosenberg thriller. We arrived in Jeddah right in the middle of Ramadan, the month in which Muslims fast during the day and then party at night. Government offices, stores, factories, taxicabs, and businesses shut down during the day, but as soon as the sun hits the horizon, a plate of dates is passed around to break the fast, and the parties begin.

The organizers booked us to stay at the Hilton in the city of Jeddah, but the event was actually almost two hours north, in a little fishing village on the Red Sea coast. We discovered that setup, sound, video checks, and rehearsals could not be carried out during the daytime because of Ramadan. We left the hotel with the other musicians and performers at 10:00 p.m., in the dark of night, and traveled for two hours north in a fleet of black SUVs to set up. Fortunately, our body clocks were still functioning on US time, so we were fairly alert. It was also cooler in the dark. We arrived at the site at midnight. The workers were preparing a huge tent to house the event. Men and women in typical Arab garb thronged around us as we unloaded and tried to set up my light table.

Everything was lit by harsh LED lights; beyond was the darkness of the desert and the sea. The tech crew was a rabble of untrained, inexperienced, lethargic guys who didn't seem interested in getting anything set up. I compounded the problem with my inability to speak Arabic. After four hours of frustrating inactivity, the drivers were ready to take us back to the hotel so we could arrive before dawn.

After about thirty minutes on the road, we noticed that our driver was beginning to nod a little and twitch the steering wheel as he snapped awake. I poked him from the back seat and asked if he was going to be able to drive. In broken English, he tried to tell us he was fine, but he did open the window halfway and turn up the radio. In a few minutes, he started to nod again. This time he shook his head and shoved the accelerator to the floor. Looking back at us, he grinned and said, and I quote, "I go slow—I sleep; I go fast—I wake."

Now we were careening through the darkness of the Arabian Desert at 120 miles per hour; I know because I could see the speedometer. Some strange mix of Arabian rock/funk music was blaring from the radio. Wind whipped through the open window. Camels and herders flashed past in a blur. Cindy had a death grip on my hand that threatened to snap small bones and prevent me from ever performing another SandStory again. Our driver was still nodding off. I yelled over the roar of the wind that I would be willing to drive, but he shook his head and said something about not having a driver's license. I was not sure if he meant me or him.

Our screaming finally got him to pull over. Ours was the only vehicle to stop. In the dark and oppressive heat, we helped our driver pour tepid water on his face and drink some Diet Coke. Maybe the caffeine would help. Cindy was sure that a band of camel-riding Al-Qaeda terrorists were just waiting to leap out of the darkness to slit the men's throats and carry the women off to some harem in the mountains. Our friends would be able to watch the whole grisly ordeal on YouTube. With a huge sigh of relief, we finally pulled up at our hotel at 6:00 a.m., dripping with nervous perspiration. Then the fasting began all over again.

We felt like we had been kidnapped and beaten. The other problem was, we were starving! All the restaurants were closed. Being the alpha male, I set off to hunt and gather for my mate. I was fortunate to find a buffet with leftovers from the nighttime revelry. With an assortment of dates, figs, and flatbread, I returned to my cave. It was enough to keep body and soul together.

Kanpur, India

One of our wildest adventures involved getting lost in downtown Lucknow, India, with a vanload of hookahs. When I tell this story, people are shocked, because they sometimes misunderstand that last word.

Tim received a call from the India Institute of Technology in Kanpur, India, to perform at their annual student-led festival. Robot wars, high-tech scavenger hunts, and various entrepreneurial endeavors were part of the celebration on the IIT campus. At the closing event, five thousand students wanted to watch the custom SandStory, but with only two thousand seats in the auditorium, I had to perform twice.

After the event, the student organizing committee invited us to the food court to share the bounty and variety of the student entrepreneurs. One of the most unusual was a "hookah parlor." Persian carpets lined the walls, and pillows littered the floor of this booth, where Muhammad, one of the students, had nine or ten hookah pipes available for rent. For those who might not know, a hookah is a water-filled smoking device that burns fruit peelings, flower petals, leaves, and tobacco, for an aromatic smoke that cools as it bubbles through a bowl of water. Five or six hoses tipped with mouthpieces snake out of the bottom for the smokers.

The hookahs, quite popular in the Middle East and India, are usually decorated with gems, engravings, and metal filigree. In keeping with the entrepreneurial theme, Muhammad had rented the pipes from a friend in the nearby town of Lucknow and was offering a smoke for ten rupees. Netting it all out, I think he was going to have a pile of rupees when it was over.

At closing time, Muhammad, who did not own a vehicle, had talked our designated driver into giving him a ride to drop off the hookahs and take him home. When it was time to take us back to the airport, Cindy, our driver, our luggage, Muhammad and his ten hookahs, and I piled into a dilapidated, noisy Land Rover. We went rattling off toward the hookah store, then to drop Muhammad off, and on to the airport.

Traffic in India is the worst and noisiest I have ever seen. Every commercial vehicle has "Please Honk" painted in big letters on the back. So everybody does. They totally ignore traffic lanes. They pass on the left, on the right, through the middle, and honk incessantly at everything that moves. Bicycles, mopeds, and scooters carrying families of five or six: Dad, Mom, and three or four kids (one in arms) wobble between cars and trucks, charging each other in oncoming lanes, honking the entire time.

And don't forget the cows. In the middle of every street, alley, and highway, wandering unfazed by the din, the holy bovine are treated like the Brahmin of India. Sometimes they were even lying asleep in the fast lane. It was *insane!*

Still on our way to the hookah store, we got lost. Or I should say our *driver* got lost. Cindy and I never did have a clue where we were. Fearing that we were going to miss our flight, we urged our driver to greater speed. He decided on back roads to get past the traffic, and soon we found ourselves in twisting alleys heaped with garbage (I think there was a strike going on) and even more cows. Suddenly we came to a dead end.

A group of large turbaned men with long, curved daggers in their waist sashes peered at us from under turbans and dark, bushy eyebrows. As Muhammad started to lower his window for directions, Cindy, in that tight, teeth-clenched, authoritative voice that I have only heard her use one other time in our marriage, said, *"Turn around* and take us to the airport *now!"*

I don't know if Muhammad got his hookahs back to the store, but from the four hundred new Facebook friends from Kanpur, India, and dozens of e-mails from new fans, it was obvious the event was a huge success. Since I lived to write this tale, you know we survived to have yet another adventure.

Bogota, Colombia

Latin American audiences are my favorite. They are as enthusiastic about my SandStory performances as they are about soccer. Our first trip to Bogota was beyond exciting. A major TV company invited us down for an exclusive party for celebrities, the media, and politicians, to celebrate the introduction of high-definition television to the Colombian market. It was held at the top of their version of the World Trade Center. Eight hundred guests, dressed to the nines, went crazy for my SandStory performance that depicted the evolution of communication and ended with a giant TV set. They dragged me around the room afterward. I was hugged, kissed, and photographed like a rock star. The next trip to Colombia, a year later, started out a little differently.

The event producer for Colombian presidential candidate Juan Manuel Santos invited me down to Bogota to perform for one of the candidates campaign rallys. He was also in charge of producing a concert for Aerosmith, a seventies rock band, scheduled at the same time. His rather devious plan was to use the Aerosmith concert and their fifty thousand fans to promote Santos. My SandStory recounting the struggles of Colombia, including the war with the revolutionaries; struggles with the drug cartels; murders, shootings, and kidnappings would end with the hopeful image of a little boy lighting a candle and close with the logo of the Santos campaign. It was a powerful but obviously political story.

Cindy and I were already in Bogota, sitting at a café, drinking mountain-grown Colombian coffee, hand-picked by Juan Valdéz. On the day of the event, we were waiting for someone to give us a setup and rehearsal time. As we drew closer and closer to concert time without a word, I started getting nervous. It was late, even by Latin American standards.

Finally the call came. I was being dissed by Aerosmith. That's right, the rock band Aerosmith didn't want me to open for them. Somebody in the Aerosmith entourage got word of the nefarious scheme to use SandStory to plug the candidate. They sent a message through the local producer. There was no way Aerosmith would be on stage with anyone endorsing any political candidate, especially Juan Manuel Santos.

It was really not a surprise, because their very next gig was for huge Aerosmith fan Hugo Chavez, the left-leaning president of Venezuela. He hated candidate Santos, the former leader of Colombian national security, because Santos kept chasing the drug lords and rebels into Venezuelan territory. Oh well. Cindy and I did get to see the rock stars up close, and they do look like very ancient lizards.

Rather than send us back to the United States without performing at all, the event producer asked us to stay on an extra day and perform at the political rally scheduled for that Friday. Okay, it wasn't going to be for the fifty thousand Aerosmith fans in an outdoor pavilion, but it was for a measly thirty-five thousand Santos fans in the Bogota Coliseum.

By the time we arrived, the fiesta was in full swing. Mariachi bands, balloons, streamers, confetti, and passionate supporters packed the Coliseum to the rafters. I set up on stage in full view of the fans, while musicians and speakers were whipping them into a frenzy. The presidential candidate had not arrived yet, so I assumed my performance would be for the fans only. Back in the green room, we were told I would be on in fifteen minutes; no, twenty-five minutes; no, the candidate just arrived. You go on now!

When I got back to the stage, there was Juan Manuel Santos, the vice-presidential candidate, and both their wives, surrounded by a couple hundred young supporters carrying "Santos Si" signs. The event planner shoved me into the crowd and said, "¡Ahora! Now!" Wedged behind my table by the chanting young people, I pushed the music cue on my iPod. The music started, and my hands appeared on three giant screens positioned over our heads.

My custom piece depicted the Colombian struggle against the FARC revolutionary forces. As the images of blindfolded captives and barbed-wire fences started appearing under my fingers, the crowd began to hush. Bombs went off, and bullets flew in my sand images. I could hear soft cries in the massive auditorium. Women began sobbing openly, and men were wiping tears from their cheeks.

The music reached a crescendo and then went soft as I began to draw the little boy holding a teddy bear. His little hand reached out, the candle lit, and a warm glow filled the screen. I encircled him with the Santos logo and dropped my hands away from the table. Pandemonium broke loose. Everyone in the place was cheering, whistling, clapping, stomping, and throwing things into the air.

Taken aback by this unbridled display of emotion, I started to slip off stage through the crowd; it was not going to happen. Three or four young guys grabbed and shoved me to center stage, next to Mr.

Santos. His wife, with tears streaming and mascara running down her face, threw her arms around me, thanking me for the beautiful story. Juan Manuel Santos grabbed one hand, the VP candidate grabbed the other and hoisted them high in the air. Cheers, whistles, clapping, and stomping washed over us from an overadrenalized, fanatical crowd.

Cindy, in the meantime, unable to find a quiet room to pray, had huddled in a corner of the holding room with dozens of band members and technicians. When she heard my music end and the roar of the crowd, she tried to make her way backstage to find me. This was the first time the vice-presidential and presidential candidates had both been on stage at the same time. Because of security concerns, armed guards were everywhere. They fended her off as she kept repeating, "¡Artista! ¡Arena! Sand artist!" To her, it sounded like mob violence, and she feared for my safety. I was sort of thinking the same thing.

Finally, candidates, wives, a handful of dignitaries, and I were carved out of the mob, surrounded with security, and squeezed backstage. Cindy, waving frantically from within the press, was pulled to safety inside the cordon. In a quiet hallway, we had a few moments to speak to Mr. Santos and his family. When Cindy told him that we had been praying for him, he and his wife seemed genuinely pleased. Photos, hugs, and handshakes all around ended the evening.

Feeling like we had just come out of the spin cycle of an industrial washing machine, Cindy and I were chauffeured back to our hotel. There in the silence, we again asked ourselves, "How in the world did we get here?" It took three days to come down from the rush of that experience. I can't affirm that President Santos got elected because of my SandStory performance … but he did get elected. Just saying.

CHAPTER NINE

CHALLENGES AND CATASTROPHES

If It Was Easy, Everyone Would Be Doing It

A good man falls seven times and gets up.
—Psalm 139:5

Breaking Glass

The surface I needed to perform on for my SandStories had to be glass. The only problem was, it would break. Or perhaps I should say airline baggage handlers would break it. Over the years, I tested dozens of space-age plastics; nothing worked. Plastic is much more susceptible to building up a static electrical charge, and the sand I use has a high metal content. The effect, of course, is sand that takes on a life of its own. With the magic of magnetism, it starts fanning out unbidden in prearranged static-electric patterns. The results can be interesting. When I draw the face of Jesus, the eyelashes look like they were applied by Tammy Faye Bakker.

Upon arrival, we immediately—right at baggage claim—open the case my light table rides in and check the glass. It's a lesson we learned the hard way. Most of the time it is fine, but if they started tossing luggage out before the luggage ramp is in place, it can get broken. A twenty-foot drop onto one corner is guaranteed to smash anything.

Cindy and I have discovered, fortunately, that glass stores are more common than McDonald's. Even more than Starbucks, if you can believe it! The challenge of finding, ordering, and picking up a piece of quarter-inch plate glass is rarely more complicated than going through the drive-thru and getting a white chocolate mocha.

Twenty thousand screaming teenagers were already finding their seats in the Thompson-Boling Arena in Knoxville, Tennessee, when we opened our case and found the glass in smithereens. I was scheduled to go on in forty-five minutes. In a panic, I grabbed my lifeline. My iPhone has become incredibly valuable in these circumstances. I googled "plate glass" and found there was a glass store only six blocks away. Immediately, I called to order an emergency twenty-by-thirty-six-inch piece. A conference volunteer scampered off to pick it up. Meanwhile, I set up and did a sound and video check, praying the entire time that the kid would not drop the glass, get lost, have a wreck, or decide to stop at the army recruiting office to sign up for a tour of duty in Iraq on the way back.

With only ten minutes to spare, the volunteer arrived with the glass. I taped it into place, my heart beating like a bike going over rumble strips and my hands shaking so I could hardly draw. The show went on. I assumed they liked it, since they stood and cheered through the entire twenty-two-minute performance. I was a wreck; Cindy was only marginally better. That was when we made the decision to *always* check the glass at the airport or with enough time to get it replaced.

Landing at the Houston airport for a performance, I opened the case to reveal broken glass. This was for a rather classy event that sent a stretch limo to pick us up. After a long explanation about what we did, we talked the reluctant uniformed driver into stopping at a glass shop on the way to the venue. I had called ahead and ordered the right size.

Google is handy for finding a glass shop but gives you no information about the sleaze factor of the neighborhood or which side of the tracks the glass store is on. Our driver started looking a little nervous when the streets got narrower, shady characters appeared on street corners, and the limo started bouncing over potholes and trash on the street. We passed the glass shop twice before we finally located it. José, the owner/glass cutter/receptionist, already had the piece cut and ready to go.

One of the other challenges of finding our glass broken is where to put the pieces—eighteen pounds of jagged, razor-sharp shards. I asked José, the owner/glass cutter/receptionist/sales clerk, if I could dump the broken pieces in his dumpster. *"Si, claro. No hay problema,"* he said. For the uninitiated, that's Spanish for "okey-dokey."

My light table case is very large and could neatly fit a dead body, if it had been cut up with a chainsaw. The three of us, me in my black performance outfit, our driver in his uniform, and José, opened the trunk of the limo, carried my light-table case around back to the dumpster, and emptied out the broken glass. I am sure that many of the unsavory characters hanging around on the street corner wondered how José had gotten involved with the Mafia and why he had to dispose of a dead body in broad daylight.

Cindy, sitting patiently in the back seat, exercising great faith, and pouring out massive amounts of prayer, could have achieved sainthood for enduring all this. She not only prays for my performances and the audience response, she also prays for safe travels, health, and no broken glass.

Plane Delays

"The plane has been slightly delayed." That sounds so innocuous; no big deal. So you get to where you want to go a little late. That just doesn't tell the whole story. An entire avalanche of events and changes cascade down each time there is a "slight delay." Especially if it is our flight! Are we going to make the event in time to perform? How long is the delay? Do we have time to get something to eat? Should we try to get another flight? Can we rent a car and drive? Will my light table get on the right plane? What is causing the delay? Did the pilot just oversleep, or is it a malfunction of the landing gear? Will they fix it? If they are under pressure, will they fix it right? Is the plane going to crash? Are we going to die?

The most catastrophic delay involved having to get on another flight. Go to a city we didn't want to go to, so we could catch a flight back to where we wanted to be in the first place. Then get on a plane that was *not* delayed and eventually get to where we were going. Our luggage, including my table, did not.

Sprinting to catch another flight is also a necessity at times. We have managed to make quite a few flights by getting our Olympic workout, dashing down an airport concourse saying, "Excuse me, excuse me, so sorry, my bad," then leaping last minute across the gap between the jet bridge and the closing door on the plane. We then stand there for a second, sweat running down our faces, with everyone else sitting quietly in their seats, looking at us, knowing they are thinking, *Who are these rubes that couldn't get out of bed early enough to get to the plane on time?*

From the beginning, we have flown Delta Airlines almost exclusively, except when they don't fly where we want to go. To their credit, our luggage has been misplaced only twice in seven years. We also have never missed an event. Weather, plane repairs, crew delays, technical difficulties, and acts of God have never prevented us from being on time and having the show go on as scheduled. Except once. Okay, twice.

Filling Out Paperwork

The only real delay was on our trip to India. In my mind, travel should be a leisurely, enjoyable affair. The airlines really work hard to try to make it just that, but governments, ahh, that is a different story. Red tape, petty bureaucrats, rubber-stamping clerks, and endless reams of documents to fill out become the norm.

When Cindy and I started performing outside the United States, we discovered the complexities of "paaaaaapuhwerk." (Pronounced that way by Roz, the giant slug in the Pixar animated movie *Monsters, Inc.* She was my favorite character in the movie.)

Passports, visas, approval documents, entry forms, and immigration forms are all "paaaaaapuhwerk." The trip to India required our passports provided by the US government and visas issued by the Indian consulate. We both had up-to-date passports but were required to send them to the Indian consulate for the visa approval.

A private company called Travisa advertised online that they could "expedite" the work of getting documents for international travel—for a fee. A substantial fee. But when you are hanging by a thread for an event that promises to be quite lucrative, you bite the bullet, suck it up, and write the check. They, indeed, were able to get things done. I don't know if the daughter of the Indian ambassador is dating the son of the friend of the neighbor of the clerk at Travisa or not, but somehow the paperwork was expedited in Washington, DC, and put in a FedEx packet to be mailed to us.

Then a huge snowstorm hit. The city of Washington shut down. The Eastern Seaboard closed its doors. The famous FedEx motto, "The World on Time," was shelved. Spending the night at my son's house in Johnson City, Tennessee, we waited for the paperwork to arrive. We had to drive to Atlanta, fly to Amsterdam, New Delhi, and finally, land twenty-two hours later in the Indian town of Lucknow. Coincidentally, we needed a little luck … *now!* The organizers agreed to postpone my performance from the beginning of the conference on Monday to the final day on Friday. Wednesday was the last day we could fly out of Atlanta and still get there on time.

Twelve inches of snow blanketed the ground in Tennessee. Washington, DC, was locked down with eighteen inches, and nobody was moving in between. We were doomed.

FedEx usually delivers overnight packages by 11:00 a.m. No FedEx, no package. Big sigh! Seconds before noon on Wednesday, the doorbell rang, and there stood the harried FedEx guy, who had braved snow and sleet and dark of night to deliver our visas. With the car already packed, we leaped in and headed for Atlanta and the grueling overnight flight to India. We arrived five days late, but we made the event.

Travisa has bailed us out numerous times with paperwork for Saudi Arabia, Qatar, Colombia, and the like, but they could not help us get into Canada. Nope. Our only real cancellation was in Canada. The Family Channel worked out the details with Tim to have us fly up and film a SandStory clip promoting the cartoon show, *Phineas and Ferb.* The Canadian customs officer in Toronto asked the purpose of our visit.

"I am filming a commercial for the Family Channel," I blurted out naively.

Hmmm. Frowns all around. He looked at me through very bushy eyebrows. "Could I see your LMO, please?"

"What is an LMO?" I asked, getting nervous.

He looked at me as if I had just flunked preschool. "A Labor Market Opinion."

"I'm sorry, I don't know what that is," I murmured humbly. I knew the fate of this trip was in his hands. Cindy, at this point, ever organized and on the ball, began producing the contract, letters from the Family Channel, letters from our agent Tim, passports, birth certificates, flight itineraries, and Google map printouts of where we were going.

The officer looked at each with a deepening frown. He shook his head. "I need the Labor Market Opinion."

An armed guard appeared as if by magic, undoubtedly summoned by some secret button the Customs officer had pushed with the toe of his shiny officer's shoes. He looked up through his eye foliage, handed the guard all our paperwork, and mumbled, "No LMO," as if we had snuck into the Customs area without any clothes on.

"Please follow me," the guard said curtly.

What ensued was profoundly embarrassing. A second armed guard fell in line behind us, and we were escorted like criminals to the baggage claim to get our luggage, then led to a locked room, where we were told to wait. Big signs on the wall declared: NO CELL PHONE USAGE!

When we were finally called to one of the six cubicles we were told that a Labor Market Opinion Form was a document that was supposed to be provided by the Family Channel, proving that a Canadian could not or would not do our job. I patiently explained to the steely-faced, uniformed matron behind the glass that there were no SandStory artists in Canada. In fact, there were none on the American continent and probably only three or four in the known universe. None of that fazed her in the least. She took the number of our contact in Canada and claimed that she would try to call. To our dismay, we learned it was Independence Day in Canada. They observe the holiday religiously, and nobody was even carrying their phones, much less answering them.

So we sat. Six hours we sat. We could not even go get food on our own. I broke every rule posted on all the walls. Hiding in the men's restroom, I called everybody I could think of. Tim was scrambling as well, but to no avail. No LMO, no go.

Finally the armed, jackbooted guards forced us to gather our belongings, marched us to the first flight back to the United States, and only handed us our passports and documents as we were stepping onto the plane. Destination: whatever US city that flight happened to go. At our own expense. Lesson learned: do the paperwork. Even if it seems ridiculous, trivial, bureaucratic, unnecessary, and redundant (as most government forms are), just do the "paaaaaapuhwerk."

CHAPTER TEN

GETTING REAL

The Real Truth about Reality Shows

For these truths are just shadows of the reality yet to come.
—Colossians 2:17

America's Got Talent?

*F*ace it: reality shows are not anything like real life. They are orchestrated, choreographed, revised, edited, and manipulated versions of what the producers want their audience to see. For three years in a row, the folks from *America's Got Talent* had called, asking for me to try out for their show. That should tell you right off that not everybody on the show stands in line for days before they are allowed to audition.

I was told that none of the performers get paid to be on television. It was a trade-off. You perform for free, but if you make it to the live rounds, you get the exposure. Once a contestant is accepted in the competition, *AGT* does provide transportation to the venue, lodging, outfits to wear, and all of thirty-five dollars per day for meals. The $1 million promised to the winner is, in reality, an annuity paid out over forty years. I would be dead before I could collect. Even knowing all that, trying out makes a great deal of sense for a talented person who doesn't have much of an audience or stage to perform on. I was not sure if I fit that category.

Being on television was never on my radar, and being a "celebrity" had no appeal whatsoever. But after the third call from *AGT*, my perceptive and clever wife suggested, "Joe, God may be opening a door that He wants you to go through."

Reluctantly, I agreed to fly to Austin, Texas, for the audition in front of the three judges: Howie Mandel, Sharon Osbourne, and Howard Stern. There was only one piece in my repertoire at the time that I felt I could condense to ninety seconds. (Yup, that was all they gave me, ninety seconds to tell an epic story). I chose a SandStory version of Lee Greenwood's "God Bless the USA."

What I figured was that Howie was Canadian, so he wasn't interested in God blessing the USA; Sharon was British, so she didn't care if God blessed the USA; and Howard was so far out, I didn't even know if he believed in God! Three Xs, and I would be done. Telling Bible stories and performing for youth conferences was what I loved doing anyway.

What happened really stunned me. At the end of my performance, all three judges stood and applauded.

Howard Stern said, "Joe, that gave me goose bumps." But of course, he had to toss in something negative as well: "Joe, I love the art. I mean, after all, how many people can tell a story in sand? But you have to get rid of the beret. I hate the French, and it is not a good look for you."

So began the banter between Howard and me that went on every time I performed on the *AGT* stage.

"Howard," I countered, "I wear a beret for a very important reason."

"Yeah, what is it?" he tossed back. So I explained the whole story about the camera angle, the flying-saucer tentacles, and needing to wear a hat.

"Wear a cowboy hat or a ball cap then. Just get rid of the beret."

To my great surprise, I got passed on to the next level. I was going to Vegas!

Rough estimates are that a total of almost five hundred thousand people try out for the producers' round of *AGT*. Twelve cities host the *AGT* cast and crew for auditions. The judges probably see twelve to fifteen hundred acts and then whittle them down to the top one hundred that go on to the judges' round, held in Las Vegas.

The competition in Vegas was not for another six weeks. The initial tryouts were taped before a live audience. For the Las Vegas rounds, each act stands before the judges without any audience. You are alone. To build the drama, they make you sweat, they keep you waiting, they don't tell you anything, they usher you from one waiting room to another, and most of all, they interview you on camera for hours.

My performance was a ninety-second piece on slavery to the song "Feeling Good," sung by Michael Bublé. After each of the acts performed for the judges, we had to wait until the next day for the results. In the holding room, the producers posted a list of the judges' favorites and a list of those probably going home.

All one hundred acts squeezed into the room and milled around in front of the listings to find their name. We were instructed by the producers to jump up and down and scream if we were on the favorites list. If we were not, we were told to demonstrate sorrow, worry, and then slink off to a solitary corner and simulate grief. Then, one at a time or in groups of two or three acts, we were trooped up from the holding room back onto the stage.

The judges, at this point, are quite critical. I was on stage with two other groups that were included in the "Variety Act" category, the Aurora Light Painters and Light Wire Theater.

"In the tryouts, when we passed you on to Las Vegas," Howard Stern commented, "we told you to 'go big or go home.' We are so disappointed in all of you. Your Vegas performances were really subpar. You let us and yourselves down. You just didn't 'up your game' like you needed to." This went on until we were all crestfallen and feeling like old, trampled-on movie popcorn.

When they had us almost weeping on the stage, Howard Stern took over and said, "So pack your bags. We are giving you one more chance. You are going to New York!"

Then, with a final dig at me, he added, "But, Joe, I am telling you—get rid of that beret!"

So, with a great flourish, I removed my beret and sent it, Frisbee-style, out to the judges' stand for Howard.

I was amazed, again, that I got passed on to the live rounds in New York City. From here on, the forty-eight acts were divided into four groups of twelve, to perform on live television at the New Jersey Performing Arts Center in Newark, New Jersey. The quarterfinals were in June and July, semifinals in August, and the grand finale in September.

In the quarterfinals, twelve acts competed each week for four weeks. Only three acts from each week would move on to the semifinals. We had to wait another six weeks. It became a grueling trek. They flew me to Newark a week before the performance for stage blocking, wardrobe, lighting, makeup, material review, and rehearsals. We worked mornings late nights and spent large chunks of time during the day sitting around waiting. Cindy came with me but I had to cover all her expenses.

As soon as I got passed on to the quarterfinals, I knew I had to create another brand-new presentation. I thought that trying to squeeze a good story into ninety seconds would be the biggest challenge, but it was not. I discovered then how show business really worked. Perhaps I had been somewhat naïve, expecting to tell the stories I wanted to tell, but after submitting six or seven suggestions for themes and having the producers turn them down, reality started to set in. After all, it was their show. They *had* to get good ratings, and they thought they knew what would work. It was frustrating having to let them decide. But God is able when we are not.

I finished up the quarterfinal drawing "The Silent Planet," about endangered species, with a large eye weeping. Nick Cannon, the host of the show, turned to me as I stepped to center stage and said, "So, Joe, whose eye is that?"

"Nick, that is obviously God's eye," I said. "He entrusted us with the care of the planet, and we have not always done a very good job."

The audience loved it. It went over pretty well with the judges too. I moved on to the semifinals.

When the producers would not allow me to tell the story of the Prodigal Son for the semifinals, in an attempt to be "wise as a serpent and harmless as a dove," I fished all the way back to a song done in 1969 called "Love One Another" by the Youngbloods. With some cajoling, they finally approved it.

The final image was to be Jesus holding a young boy; they didn't like that. During rehearsals, the producers strongly suggested I remove the beard, so I did. Without the beard, it looked like a generic white guy hugging a little boy. But once I got on stage on live television, I thought, *What the heck. I am going to draw Jesus and let the chips fall.*

That is what I did. The audience again responded very enthusiastically.

A most interesting discussion ensued. Howard Stern spoke up. "That is a cool drawing, Joe, but who is that supposed to be?"

Sharon turned to Howard and responded, disgustedly, "Howard, that is Jesus."

"That is not Jesus!" he claimed.

Then Howie Mandel chimed in. "Look, Howard is Jewish. He wouldn't recognize Jesus if he saw Him."

Sharon piped up, "Well, Jesus was Jewish. Joe, wasn't Jesus Jewish?"

I nodded. "Yes, Jesus was Jewish."

Then Howard turned back to me and said, "Joe, is that supposed to be Jesus?" At this point, he was looking a little flustered.

"Howard," I said, "the beauty of artwork is that you see in it what you need to see."

The buzz on Twitter, Facebook, and my e-mails went on for days. The producers decided, America voted, and I moved on to the finals.

The reason given most often for rejecting a SandStory I wanted to tell was that *AGT* was not able to get the TV rights for a certain piece of music. From the very beginning, the story I had visualized doing for the finale was "Never Forget," my version of the 9/11 attack. It was a powerful piece, and the music, composed for me by Doug Kaufman, a wonderfully talented friend, eliminated the need for getting TV approval, since I owned the rights. The finale, to be held on September 12 in Newark, New Jersey, was right across the river from where the World Trade Center towers had stood. My final image was of the I-beam cross discovered in the ruins. I had developed the presentation for the tenth anniversary of the attack and knew it was a powerful story. The message, the time, and the venue were all perfect. But it was not to be. The NBC Standards and Practices Board did not approve.

With a great deal of frustration, I told my producer, "Look, I have submitted all I have. What do you want me to do?"

I even sent notes to every *AGT* e-mail address I could find. It annoyed my producer but got no results.

At that point I was told, "We saw the cartoon that you did of Howard Stern. What about doing cartoons of the three judges?"

Reluctantly, I had to acquiesce.

Creating a likeness is one of the most difficult things an artist can try to do. Drawing the three judges in ninety seconds was almost impossible, but I had no other good options in the short time left. I was willing to give it a try. I started by presetting Nick Cannon, morphed him into a bald Howie, turned Howie into Sharon, and finished up with Howard Stern and his mass of curly hair. The final touch was putting a beret on him. It was truly ironic when Sharon Osbourne commented as I finished the cartoons, "Joe, I wish you had done something more spiritual."

America voted. At the results show the next night, I came in fifth. Even though I was not allowed to perform what I wanted, I am convinced that I wound up right where God wanted me to be. After it was all said and done, the experience was a reminder that we can make our plans, but God guides our steps.

Backstage Ministry

Only God will know what came of the spiritual seeds planted because of the TV exposure. In the following months, many hundreds of people spotted me in restaurants, hotel lobbies, and airports and commented on the impact my SandStories had on them. Although I was prevented from telling the stories I wanted to tell on camera, backstage was a different story. Cindy and I had numerous opportunities to encourage, share, and pray with some of the young *AGT* staff and the other performers.

My favorite memory involves The Untouchables. Thirty young kids, ages nine to thirteen, made up the Miami-based dance troupe. Talented, hard-working, and mostly Hispanic, these were fresh-faced kids I related to immediately because of my Mexican roots and ability to speak Spanish.

During one of the interminable waits in the green room, The Untouchables and I were the only two acts left. I was sitting on one of the couches with two young guys on either side. My iPhone has become my spiritual resource, and I was using an app that gives you the verses to read through the Bible in a year. Justin, seated on my left, leaned in, and with the typical curiosity of a thirteen-year-old, asked, "Whatcha reading?"

"I am reading the Bible," I answered.

"Hey, cool! Can I see?"

He took my iPhone and, being technically savvy like most his age, started punching different apps.

"Whoa, dude! You have eight Bible apps on your phone. How come you have so many Bibles?"

I smiled (both inside and out). "That's easy. I believe that the Bible is God's instruction manual and manufacturer's warranty for planet Earth. If we want to know how to navigate life successfully, we need to read the handbook."

"Man, that is interesting. Like, what sort of stuff does it tell you?" he asked, clearly interested.

"Well, for one, it tells us in the book of Proverbs how to handle fame and success without letting it go to our heads and ruining our lives."

His eyes widened. "Does it really say that?"

"Sure, that and much more. It talks about how to pick a wife, how to have a successful marriage, how to handle money, and what to do with it. It gives us all kinds of valuable information."

Then Mario, who was on my right, leaned over and asked, "I heard there were all kinds of translations of the Bible. How can you know which one is the right one to read?"

I gave a brief synopsis of Bible translations and how to pick a good one. At that point, some of the young girls sitting on the floor scooted up to the couch and started asking questions. As I gave succinct answers that I had been giving in youth meetings for more than thirty years, the questions just kept coming. More of the kids gathered close. The questions started becoming more theological.

"If God is supposed to be a loving God, why does so much bad stuff always happen?" asked one sharp young girl. That was fun trying to answer.

A ten-year-old girl asked, "My grandmother just died two weeks ago. Can I know if she went to heaven?"

That question opened the opportunity to share the gospel in a simple and understandable way. By this time, about fifteen of The Untouchables were sitting around, just like at the old Bible studies I used to have in Pompano, Florida, when I was in Bible college.

"Yes, we know that we can go to heaven. Jesus explained that to a rich guy named Nicodemus one night when he snuck over to where Jesus was staying," I told them. "'If you believe in me,' said Jesus, 'you can know that you have eternal life.'"

Somebody asked if prayer really worked. I told them about the double-blind study done at the Mayo Clinic, where people in intensive care were prayed for without their knowledge and improved significantly faster than those who were not.

At that point, I looked up.

Manuel, the director of the dance troupe, whom they called Manny, was across the green room watching the unfolding discussion with the kids. His eyes met mine. I was uncertain how he would react. A small nod, a smile, and a thumbs-up sign told me he approved. After forty-five minutes of impromptu Bible study and Q-and-A, the assistant to the producer stuck his head in the door and announced, "Untouchables, you are next on stage."

With the pent-up energy that is so abundant in young people, they jumped to their feet, fussing with their outfits, and started gathering at the door. Justin, the young man who started it all, leaped to his feet and announced loudly, "Wait! Everyone come here. I want to pray before we go on stage."

The AGT Aftermath

Before the last of the confetti drifted down on the final night, before all the audience had gone and the lights were turned out, the top six finalists were snagged as we walked offstage and reminded we had obligations to keep. The 130-page contract we had signed before we had ever made it to see the judges made it clear that we were to be available for an undisclosed number of performances, to be set by FremantleMedia, the producers of *AGT Live*. The producers of the *Live* stage show told us we were going to be part of a show, six nights a week, at the Palazzo Theatre in Las Vegas. The show was to run from mid-September through Thanksgiving and resume in January for another eight weeks. Rehearsals were to begin in three days.

Three days? Cindy and I hadn't been home in three *weeks!* That would not have given us enough time to do our laundry, much less pack for an eight-week stay in Las Vegas. With much wheedling and cajoling, Tim, our agent, managed to buy us four extra days. One week after the final night of the *AGT* televised show, we were getting on a plane for Vegas.

For this, we did get paid. It was less than we could earn performing at our going rate, but we were provided with very nice accommodations, with full kitchens and hot tubs at the Grand View Resort. We were also given a stipend for groceries, our own dressing rooms, rental vehicles to share, and a place in the Palazzo Hotel to sell merchandise.

The first two weeks were rough. The TV show had a significant budget, with hundreds of stagehands, technical people, runners, helpers, makeup, costume designers, and seamstresses. The live

Las Vegas show, not so much. About twelve people were producing, directing, running lights, sound, stage changes, props, wardrobe, and everything else involved. Cues were missed, timing was off, and props didn't always work. On top of that, not all of the top six contestants were in the show.

The winners, Olate Dogs, got top billing. William Close and the Earth Harp Collective, Tom Cotter, the comedian, and I were four of the finalists. Semifinalists, Lightwire Theatre and Spencer Horseman, the escape artist, were brought in, and Recycled Percussion, a drumming group from season five filled out the roster.

We enjoyed working at a slower pace, since we performed the same material every night. We got to know the other performers. Occasional parties and outings gave us opportunities to interact and have longer conversations with them. They were congenial and hard-working people.

Eight weeks in Las Vegas is a long time. Although Cindy and I tried to integrate, find a church, and make friends, most people lived a fast-paced lifestyle. We didn't want to move that fast. After six weeks, Cindy had had enough. She decided to head back for Kentucky and leave me to wrap up the last two weeks on my own. She wanted me to finish well.

Finishing well included filling out the paperwork terminating our relationship with FremantleMedia, so we could get back to what we were doing before. We were very relieved when it was all done.

CHAPTER ELEVEN

NO TRANSLATION REQUIRED

How Do You Say This in Sand?

Now the whole world had one language and a common speech.
—Genesis 11:1

Opportunities to Share

*A*rt is often referred to as a universal language. I have discovered this to be true in a special way, particularly if it is used to tell a universal story. Those stories that touch us most deeply are true for everyone in the whole world—stories of love, of hope, of faith; stories of failure, brokenness, and redemption. They can touch the soul of every being on the planet who has eyes to see and ears to hear. You see, humans were created to have a relationship with their Creator. All people, at some point, have failed and broken that relationship, but God, demonstrating His great mercy, offered us restoration through His Son, Jesus. This is the story that will touch us all.

In Detroit, Michigan, I performed two services at a medium-sized church. I thought we were done. Not so, the pastor said. He asked me to perform at an afternoon meeting for Asian families. Thirteen years earlier, the church had started a ministry to the wives of Asian executives who were traveling to Detroit because of the auto industry. The men were learning the language and assimilating well because of being in the work environment. The wives were not.

What began as an afternoon tea for these women turned into ESL classes, shopping expeditions, Bible studies, and two annual events for the entire family. The women often asked why the members of the church were being so kind to them with nothing expected in return. Christmas and Easter were perfect seasons to illustrate what motivated this unconditional love: the basics of Christianity.

The church invited the Asian families to learn about the Easter holiday. Four hundred Asians, wielding more cameras and video equipment than a Best Buy store, gathered in the church gym. Chairs were brought in, until there was standing room only. The pastor then began one of the oddest sermons I had ever heard. He gave a welcome in English, and a translator reiterated it in Japanese, Korean, and Mandarin. He then turned to me, and instead of laboriously translating his comments into three different languages, he introduced me. I shared the Christian story of Easter in the sand.

There was no doubt in my mind that the audience understood the stories, and the impact was great. It dawned on me at that point that my stories could be told anywhere in the world.

Although I usually create corporate SandStories specifically for each event without spiritual content, I am continually amazed at the numerous opportunities I have had and continue to have to share the good news in far-flung pockets of the globe.

On one of our trips to the Middle East, we spent long hours standing around, waiting for tech people to get the sound and lights working. Needing to do something with the time, I sauntered over to our drivers, who spoke a smattering of English but were not fluent by any measure. On each vehicle, a huge decal made up of Arabic writing over two crossed swords covered the entire back window.

"So, what does that say?" I asked.

One of the most vocal of the drivers proudly pointed to his decal and said, "It says Allah is one, and Mohammed is his prophet."

It occurred to me that I too have a decal on the back of my vehicle. It is a tiny fish, hidden down low on the left side of my bumper. So much for my boldness in proclaiming the gospel in my own country, where they don't behead infidels for identifying with Christ. In the oppressive Ramadan heat at about 3:00 a.m., I shared what Christ meant to me. When Cindy found me an hour later, I was surrounded by half a dozen turbaned Arabs, listening to me defend the resurrection of Christ.

Many times, the event planners are people who are progressive and curious about our Western ways. They also are often very interested in improving their English. I hand out gospels of John that I get from the Pocket Testament League, which are usually received with appreciation and a promise to read them. I do remember a few times when all I got was an icy stare in conjunction with a slow side-to-side head shake. Who knows? Some seeds might have been planted in those desert sands. Not until we are in heaven will we have any idea of what seeds fell by the wayside and which ones produced a hundred fold.

Milan, Italy is considered to be a sophisticated fashion center and manufacturing hub. It is also the home of some of the most wonderful Christian artwork in the world. A large European telephone conglomerate invited me there to perform for three hundred of their top salespeople. They left the topic of the SandStory up to me.

As I mingled with them prior to the performance, I discovered that most of them could not speak English. My Italian consists entirely of items gleaned from Olive Garden menus. Communication can only go so far with gestures and cryptic phrases. I am always looking for ways to affirm, encourage, and point people to God.

Earlier in the day, Cindy and I had gotten a chance to stand before one of those iconic pieces of artwork. Leonardo da Vinci, in 1498, finished his magnificent wall-size fresco of *The Last Supper*. As we enjoyed gazing at this spectacular painting, we heard around us hushed comments in dozens of different languages. It occurred to me, the story has not changed, just the medium.

That night, before an audience who could not understand what I said, I told the story of Jesus in sand, and they understood it. The intense eye contact, moist eyes, firm two-handed handshakes, and heartfelt embraces told me clearly that they understood the message. Sand required no translation.

I have already mentioned our wild adventure in Kanpur, India. Most of the students at the India Institute of Technology spoke English because of the desire to eventually get jobs in the United States. Most of them were Hindu, with a significant segment of Muslims. When I asked what sort of SandStory they wanted me to tell, the student-body president and coordinator of the event specifically asked me if I would do "The Passion of the Christ."

My program consisted of a few short SandStories and an extended custom piece that incorporated some of the iconic images of India: elephants, tigers, temples like the Taj Mahal, and a bespectacled Mahatma Gandhi. I concluded with "The Passion." The applause for the short pieces and the story of India were thunderous, but at the end of "The Passion," they stood and cheered.

The stage was flooded with enthusiastic well-wishers, but it was Cindy who had the most fascinating conversation. A student who introduced himself as Samson made some small talk and then got around to revealing his faith by saying, "Please tell your husband to continue telling the story of Jesus until He returns." What an encouragement to know that God is at work in the most unlikely of places.

Since then, I have been able to use Google Translator on many e-mails from non-English-speaking countries. They comment on the impact of the spiritual stories, understood because they are told in sand. In any language, the right picture really is worth a thousand words.

CHAPTER TWELVE

Jet-Setting and the Glamorous Life

"Are you living the dream?"

I learned the secret, both to abound and to be in want.
—Philippians 4:12

One of our recent trips involved seven performances in three states and two countries. It had been a long, exhausting two weeks, with broken glass, a few delayed flights, and some sleepless nights. We were worn out. Our plane leveled off over the prettiest approach in the United States. White picket fences gathered in cantering thoroughbred horses, and the bluegrass of Kentucky welcomed us home. As we dragged our briefcases off the jetway, a good friend, fresh as a daisy, spotted us on his way to the gate, where he was leaving for a short speaking engagement. I don't think he travels much.

"Hey, Castillos," he gregariously shouted across the concourse. "Are you livin' the dream?"

Living the dream, indeed! Some things can feel abrasive when you are hungry, worn out, and desperately need to use the restroom.

I felt like saying, "How about I poke you in the snoot and stuff that in your dream, buddy?"

What others often see as a glamorous, jet-setting life, on occasion becomes tedious and wearisome. There are even a few times we have wanted to chuck it all and stay home. Since that day, when the going gets really tough, Cindy can almost always lighten my mood by cheerfully quoting our friend. "Well, Joe, are you livin' the dream?"

Cindy works hard to carve out some extra time, so we can rest and enjoy the places we stay. Most of the time, when we perform, we don't get to choose the hotels. They are usually very nice places, and many of them are outstanding. But not always.

A second-rate little chain motel in Gatlinburg, Tennessee, looms large in my memory. Every room in the whole town was taken, and the guy planning the event had booked us in the only room available, at this motel. It was that or sleep in our car.

My first clue that something was wrong was that all the potted plants in the lobby were dead. Well, two of them were. The other one was plastic. The guy behind the desk spoke only rudimentary English, and although they had signs everywhere declaring it to be a smoke-free facility, it was obviously not. To this day, I am convinced that the pillows were stuffed with used cigarette butts.

All night long at the magnificent motel, doors slammed, music played, TVs blared, and there was at least one domestic dispute that required police intervention. At 5:30 a.m., we finally dragged our bedbug-bitten bodies back on the road for another two events. Well, OK, I may have exaggerated a bit about the bedbugs. But if there had been any, at least we could have played kill the bedbugs, for some late-night entertainment, since it seemed as if every one elses TV was working fine. Our cable TV was on the fritz.

There was no lightening the mood at that point. When we got home, our suitcases had to be left out in the garage, fumigated, and each item of clothing aired out and carried into the laundry room with rubber gloves. Ahhhh, no matter how lush or lousy the current hotel, home is always best.

Any vocation that requires travel, flexibility, long delays, uncertain schedules, and forced immobility demands Pollyanna-level cheerfulness. But an overly cheerful suggestion can instantly turn your traveling partner's frustrated annoyance into a full-blown, vitriolic outburst.

After a huge performance, we had stayed too long at our merchandise table, answering questions and autographing DVDs. We needed to catch an early-morning flight out of Oklahoma City or Oakland or Okinawa, I can't remember which. Our very cheerful hostess decided that she wanted to "make it special" and drive us to the airport, rather than have us rent a car or take a shuttle. She then filled the hour-and-a-half drive to the airport, chattering at 120 words per minute, with gusts of up to 150. Our Chatty Cathy force-fed us information we didn't want to hear, asked questions that we had already answered a *bazillion times*, and played tour guide in a town that we really never wanted to come back to.

In the back seat, Cindy almost had a seizure. All I could see was the whites of her eyes. I expected foam to start dribbling out of her mouth. At this point, our Christian testimony was at stake, so we smiled, murmured, "How true," at the end of every sentence, and prayed for no traffic jams.

Audience overload eventually affects any performer. The clinical term we have given this malady is being "peopled out." The human psyche can only answer the same questions so many times before the brain just comes to a screeching halt and says, "I don't think I am going to tell that person how I started doing sand art. I am going to put a demented look on my face and stare at their belt buckle until they get creeped out and go away."

Cindy and I have found that many performers we meet backstage in the green room never do go out and meet the audience. You would be surprised at some of the well-known Christian artists who have zero tolerance for their fans. They pay others to sell their merchandise and just don't do autographs. I personally feel a great sense of responsibility to those who want to share their stories with us or hear a little more of our own. I have shared some of the stories of how something as simple as a word or two can change a life. So Cindy and I ask God for grace and, as much as we are able, we let people in.

The reason I travel, perform, meet, and interact with people is because the message of Christ is for all people. Some celebrity status goes along with anyone who has the privilege of being on stage. It is important to know how to do that well. Jesus handled the press of the crowd in a way that gives us an example. He was never stuck on Himself, yet had great compassion for those in need. He took time to be alone with the Father, recharging His emotional batteries through prayer between those energy-sapping events with hundreds of people wanting a piece of Him. I pray regularly that people will see a little of Him in me.

Knowing When to Say When

Many sincere people needing help will text, write, or call me. Some look into my eyes at an event, hoping I can give them a word of encouragement or affirmation. Many want us to come perform at their meeting.

A pastor who claimed to know me from my college days more than forty years ago posted a request on my Facebook page: "Hey, Joe, so good to hear about your recent success. God has prompted me to contact you about performing at our church. We are small but our people are very generous and I know that they would bless you with a substantial love offering."

I was drawing a blank. At times, I don't remember who I met before lunch. I sent the information to Tim. He communicated with the pastor, who then responded, not to Tim, but to me on Facebook: "Hi, Joe, your agent said you needed [this amount] before you could perform but I know you are not in this just for the money. God would be honored if you would perform here. I have a spare bedroom in my home and we could feed you and take care of your transportation expenses. I really would not have contacted you if God had not prompted me to do so. We are totally flexible with the date so just let me know when you want to come."

I had not gotten the same memo from God.

What made this request even more awkward was the reality that I was now getting requests like this on a weekly basis. Nonprofits wanted me to perform at charity events. Christian organizations doing fundraisers were looking for a "name" that would bring people in.

Schools needed inspirational speakers and performers for chapels. Churches that had lost pastors wanted someone to fill the pulpit. Some guy wanted me to do a SandStory to propose to his girlfriend. A singer-songwriter wanted me to develop a SandStory to promote her new song. Some wanted donations. Some were just people who, in some way, wanted to have a small glow of limelight rub off on them. Being in demand is a great thing. It is also taxing.

What I do with all these requests is forward them to Tim Grable. Fortunately, Tim deflects most of the requests I can't fulfill. It's what we have in our contract, and it has worked effectively for seven years. Tim negotiates the performances. Cindy and I get to decide.

Sometimes, however, I need to do what I can to help.

Jamie waited until he was the last one standing at my table at a recent performance. Tall, angular, twenty-something, with a shaved head and a gaunt and hungry look on his face, he shared his story with tears in his eyes. He apologized for the tears and started to put on his dark glasses. I stopped his hand.

"No need to apologize. Tears are God's way of allowing us to express emotion. Let them flow. It doesn't bother me."

His story included addictions, family issues, suicide attempts, and finally shaving his head, to identify with his estranged father, who was battling cancer. He was an artist. He asked if I would be willing to counsel and mentor him.

"No, Jamie," I said, "you need to find someone here, in this church, that will help you. My schedule would not allow me to do that."

We talked, and I prayed with him. As I began to move away, he said one more thing: "I really like your beret. I wanted to buy one at your table, but your wife said you were sold out." So I gave him my beret. I could do that.

CHAPTER THIRTEEN

PRACTICAL TIPS AND IDEAS

How to Use SandStories in Your Church or Group

Jesus always used stories and illustrations like these.
—Matthew 13:34

Opening Discussions

SandStory performances and videos have proven to be effective in touching people in powerful and life-changing ways. Here are some of the methods you can use to communicate the most important message of all time in a captivating way without being threatening. C. S. Lewis talked about the power of the arts being a vehicle that could "steal past the watchful dragons." What he meant was that using the strong images created by the arts—which include music, writing, drama, painting, and now all forms of digital images—can circumvent the defenses unbelievers have placed between themselves and faith.

Art can often reach people that words cannot. I love the story told by one of the most ardent defenders of the Christian faith today. Lee

Stroble was a hard-bitten, cynical newspaper columnist for the *Chicago Tribune.* His wife had become a Christian and began inviting him to attend church with her at Willow Creek Community Church. Lee attended, sat in the back, and later groused about the sermons on the way home. One Sunday, the church played a short video, using a little animated clay figure that had a question mark appear above his head when he had questions about God. In a way Lee couldn't explain, he identified with the little clay figure. He realized, "That is me!"

The artwork had an impact in a way words could not. It was not too long until he began asking questions that led to answers and eventually to his becoming a full-blown follower of Christ. Today he is the author of numerous books defending the truths of Christianity.

I have often said, "Art is the finger of God that touches the soul."

Because the SandStory images cannot be frozen in place, cast in polymer, or glued to the glass, the only way to preserve them is with video capture. Very early in the SandStory process, I started videotaping the performances and putting them on DVDs. People who purchased them found many different ways they could be used in worship and inspirational services. The DVDs even helped people in Bible studies engage in discussions that helped them better understand the Scriptures and grow spiritually.

A father came up to our merchandise table after one of my performances and told me how his daughter had used the DVDs to share the gospel with about twelve of her friends. She planned a slumber party and invited the girls over for the night. After food, games, and the silliness that goes along with teenage gatherings, things were slowing down a little, and she asked, "Hey, y'all want to see something really cool I saw last week? I saw a guy perform this sand thing at a conference."

She then popped "The Passion" SandStory into the DVD player and turned it on. The father went on to tell me what his daughter had described happened next.

"She told me that the girls sat entranced for the entire DVD, only punctuating the soundtrack with an occasional 'Wow!' As soon as it was over, they all started talking at once. They talked about Jesus and the gospel until four o'clock in the morning."

"My daughter," said the dad, "feels like at least two of the girls came to Christ that night."

Two years ago, Augsburg Fortress Press, the publishing arm of the Lutheran Church, contacted me about creating SandStory videos for their new Bible study, *The Greatest Story.* I created a series of three DVDs: *The Story of the Word*, *The Story of Jesus*, and *The Story of Paul.* All of them were captivating, inspirational, engaging images that led people into the study of the Bible. The SandStory provided a different perspective on the lesson at hand. The series is available from *AusbergFortress.org*

Many pastors, youth workers, and Sunday school teachers have shared with us how they have used the SandStory DVDs and downloadable SandStory Snippets to point people toward Christ. I have listed some of the ways below.

Practical Ideas

1. Sermons—Start a sermon with a SandStory Snippet that triggers images in the mind of the congregation, to help cement the lesson in their memory.

2. Classes—Ask a series of questions that can be highlighted by showing one of the video Snippets. Or do it the other way around. Show the Snippet, and then ask questions about the story and what it means to us today.

3. Worship—Pick a SandStory Snippet that ties in with one of the songs the group is singing. The images reinforce the message of the lyrics and create a powerful impact. Sitting in silent contemplation after a SandStory video is also a powerful way to initiate worship.

4. Communion—Share a part or the entire SandStory video, and then, before people partake of Communion, have a station with a SandStory table, where people write in the sand. (See the instructions on how to make one in the next chapter.) They can write about issues they are dealing with, sins for which

they need forgiveness, or the name of someone they need to forgive. They can wipe the sand away, even as Christ wiped away our sins by His death on the cross.

5.   Prayer—In the same way that my wife, Cindy, sets specific times for prayer that is so effective in my ministry, set times of prayer interspersed with short SandStory Snippets that reflect the needs that are being lifted up to the Lord in prayer. Use a SandStory table to write prayer requests or personal needs.

6.   Art—Most of all, let me encourage you to be aware of God's leading and inspiration concerning the arts. The arts, well presented or performed in the right context, always point people to God.

Someone asked me once, "If art is so important, why did Jesus never paint a painting or have a one-man show?" I answered, "Oh, you are so wrong. God's art gallery is around us every minute. In the beauty and artistry of Creation, we see the glory and majesty of God, the artist. Every time Jesus pointed to a flower, a sunset, a seed, a tree, or a little child, He was presenting His art for His followers to see and appreciate."

Live Performances

Invariably, the live performances are the most powerful. When the audience realizes that I am actually on stage creating the images that appear on the screen, the impact is significantly greater. A large part of this impact comes when people see the first image and know it is changing into something else. Their minds are captivated with the mystery of what is going to come next. Even very young children understand that a story is unfolding, and they want to know how it turns out. I have lost count of the performances where invitations or opportunities to make spiritual decisions had amazing results. Gospel presentations where hundreds have indicated a decision to receive

Christ, commitment services where half the congregation will respond to rededicate their lives to Christian service and conferences where everyone in attendance will stand in a unified demonstration of their faith in Christ, are common.

The spiritual force behind the stories in Scripture creates a double impact. Many identify with the character in the Bible story or parable that brings them face to face with the message God intended them to hear. It is a thrill to watch God at work.

Just Some of the SandStories in My Repertoire

"The Passion" (10 min. or 20 min.)
A dramatic depiction of the betrayal, beating, crucifixion, and resurrection of Christ, performed to the powerful music of Mel Gibson's motion picture, *The Passion of the Christ*. This presentation has been used effectively as an outreach and evangelistic presentation.

"Creation" (10 min. or 20 min.)
Six days of Creation, including plants, fish, birds, animals, ending with the creation of Adam and Eve. This presentation is wonderful for children as well as adults.

"The Miracle of Christmas" (10 min. or 20 min.)
From the appearance of the angel to Mary, Mary and Joseph's travel to Bethlehem, ending with the birth in the stable, this is a touching story for the Advent season. This presentation has been used effectively as an outreach and evangelistic presentation.

"The Prodigal" (10 min.)
The struggle of willfulness, rebellion, and failure, overshadowed by the power of God's grace, forgiveness, and love is based on the parable of the prodigal son. This performance can be used as a time of restitution and healing.

"Around the World for Christ" (10 min. or 20 min.)
A visit to many of the world's countries and cultures ends in the vision from the book of Revelation, where people from every tribe, nation, and language bow before the throne of Christ.

"My Lord's Prayer" (4 min.)
Based on the best-known prayer in the entire world, this performance illustrates the Lord's Prayer in a unique way and touches people with the beauty of the words, the music, and magical sand animations.

"A Baby Changes Everything" (5 min.)
A touching SandStory of the song by Faith Hill about how much a pregnancy and a child change things, and the eternal change made by the birth of Christ. Used in fundraisers and awareness seminars for pregnancy counseling centers and rallies.

"God Bless the USA" (4 min.)
Still one of my most popular performances, Lee Greenwood's classic patriotic song done in sand with images of the flag, our finest young soldiers, ends with the Statue of Liberty.

"Celebrate Life" (8 to 12 min.)
A SandStory presenting joy, hope, fun, and happiness, depicting people enjoying all the stages of life.

"Parables" (12 min.)
Four of Christ's best-known parables illustrated in sand: The Wedding Feast, The Talents, The Mustard Seed, and The Parable of the Yeast, each illustrated in three-minute vignettes.

New Stories and Worship Sets

Check our website, *JoeCastillo.com*, for new SandStories and Snippets of current worship songs, music, and illustrations of Scripture passages. SandStory can be performed with your musician or worship team.

Custom Live Performances

Original SandStory performances can be custom-created for existing compositions or original music scores by request. These custom SandStory presentations can include your own images, logos, and themes.

If you are interested in having a performance for your event, please contact:
Tim Grable
615-300-3930
tim@thegrablegroup.com

So You Want to Be a SandStory Artist?

At almost every performance, someone comes over, explains that they are an artist, and wants to know how they can learn how to do sand art. Many are parents with talented children already demonstrating a desire to exhibit their creativity.

I know that sharing this information might create a barrage of sand artists to compete with my work. I am not at all concerned about that, for three reasons. First, I really do have a desire to encourage young artists to find their medium and feel fulfilled in what they do. If it happens to be sand stories, so be it. I would be most pleased to find others who want to use their abilities to tell stories about God and His work in our lives.

Secondly, any determined, curious artist can do this and figure it out on their own.

Last of all, this is a very big world. Since I developed my version of SandStory, I have seen numerous other talented artists pop up on YouTube and begin to make their mark. I have worked very hard to learn and perfect my SandStories, and competition in the ranks is a really good thing. Eventually, there will be many, many sand-art dabblers, but to perform, to be really good at anything, requires hundreds, perhaps thousands of hours of practice and performance. Many thousands of people play the cello, but there is only one Yo-Yo Ma. The Yo-Yo Ma of sand art might be reading this right now.

Creating a SandStory Light Table

The easiest way to get started working in sand is to make a trip to your local art-supply, super-department store, or hardware store, to purchase what you need. With a small, hand-held video camera and a tripod, you can get everything else for about $100 or less. If you already have a light box, used in graphic arts or photography, that works fine. If not, purchase a square, fluorescent kitchen light fixture. Usually you can find something about thirty inches square, with a smooth surface and white plexiglass cover.

In the picture-frame department, find a frame about the same size as your light fixture. Get one with a high lip or edge on it, so the sand does not spill off as easily. Go to the craft department and find a small bag of sand. You only need about two or three pounds. Almost any kind of fine-grain sand will work.

When you get home, remove the picture and mat from the frame and secure the glass so it will not fall out of the frame. Please remember, particularly if you have small children, that glass is breakable. Broken glass will cut you, and blood will not improve your SandStory images.

After setting your light fixture on a table, find a stable way of fixing your frame to the light fixture. If the fixture is flat, some duct tape will probably work. Scatter a small amount of sand on the glass, and begin experimenting with your designs.

To perform for an audience, you will need a tripod that is higher than your head and a small, hand-held video camera. You will have to place the tripod with camera behind you, so that it is centered directly over the picture frame and the image will not be upside down. If you have a camera with a composite or HDMI output, you can plug it into your television set, and voila! Watch yourself create your first SandStory.

If you want to perform for a larger audience, you can plug your camera into a digital projector, to show on a large screen. You will need the right length and proper cables for TV or digital-projector viewing. Happy SandStorying!

CHAPTER FOURTEEN

TELLING YOUR STORY

Can Your Story Make a Difference?

A word spoken at the right time is like a golden apple in a silver frame.
—Proverbs 25:11

*D*uring a real vacation to some faraway place, devoid of the usual entertainment, I discovered a free lending library with a small, thumbtacked sign that read, "Leave a book, take a book." In rummaging through the eclectic pile of well-used, soft- and hardback books, I came across one with a very interesting cover. I have to admit that many of my choices with books and other things are made by the design on the label or cover. I casually picked it up, and after reading the author's bio on the back, the synopsis on the flyleaf, and the chapter titles, I started on page one. By page two, I was hooked.

I continued to read all afternoon, all evening, and long into the night. It was a real cliffhanger. Somewhere in the gray light of early dawn, tension in the story had been ratcheted up to a frantic point. Completely engrossed as I was in the book, my heart was literally pounding in my chest. I turned what I thought was the last page. *No!* The last few pages had been ripped out! I was frantic. At that point, I would have run out in my pajamas and found a bookstore to buy a complete copy and read the rest of the story.

Too often, certain parts of our lives come to a screeching halt. Events come crashing in that make no sense, and life spirals out of control. It is at those times we look back and wonder if any of the disparate segments we have lived through have any common thread. What benefit is there in going through some of those difficulties? What can we learn from those situations? I know that I have sometimes felt that if God was writing my story, He wasn't paying very close attention.

Many of the best books, both fiction and nonfiction, that I have read in my continual search for good stories were narratives that left most of the questions unanswered until the very end. Sometimes authors even used an epilogue to tie up all the loose details. God works that way. Most of the time, we do not see His hand at work, but we can always trust His heart. His love for us is inexhaustible. His ability to know it all is complete. His power to work everything together for our good is sure. I am convinced that every life story will end with a knowledge that God is transparently just. He is unquestionably fair. He brings every detail to a satisfactory conclusion.

This book is a very small attempt to piece together a quilt of my own experiences, stitched together with God's precise needlepoint. I still see most of the quilt from the back side, where stitching and knots abound. I am unable to see the finished work. But the beauty of the completed pattern is beginning to show through. It fills me with an overwhelming glow of gratitude at the beautiful, intricately cut pieces being fit together each year as I draw closer to the final chapter. Not that I am in any way ready to hang up my bag of sand. I will keep living the story until my patient Author, Creator, Artist is done.

We can't write the end of our own story, but we are responsible for sharing what we have learned with others. The Bible makes it very clear that we are to proclaim how God has worked in our lives and the salvation available in Christ.

His promise is that by faith, we can be forgiven for all our failures, given the power to lead a new life, and given the assurance of a home in heaven after death. Jesus made these bold and audacious claims. "In my name you can be forgiven for your sins." Mark 9:2 "Come to me and I will give you rest." Matthew 11:28. "Believe in me and you will have eternal life." John 3:16

Those fulfilled promises should become a significant part of our story. The best way to share that good news is by telling people about it as we have experienced it, never forced, awkward, or fake. The apostle Paul told his story everyplace he went. "I was on the road to Damascus ..." is not only recorded in the Scriptures but has become a part of our language. Most people know what a "Damascus road" experience is.

Our story does not have to be dramatic or sensational. It just needs to be true and told sincerely from the heart. People will be changed, not by the drama of the story or the clever way we tell it. They will be changed by the power of God behind the truth of the story.

I often tell people about Moses. He had a staff. By all I can determine, it was just a stick, a piece of wood. But when he was willing to turn it over to God, it was transformed into a powerful tool for rescuing God's people, parting the Red Sea, changing the heart of Pharaoh, and bringing water from a rock for thirsty people. All of those miraculous events came from an ordinary stick.

What do you have in *your* hand? What is your story? What can you say to help rescue people from guilt, fear, loneliness, and despair?

All I had was a handful of ordinary, common sand.

CPSIA information can be obtained at www.ICGtesting.com
Printed in the USA
LVOW11s0814101214

418093LV00001B/1/P